The Long Way Home

*The Collected Short Stories
& Other Bruises
of Frank Howson*

It's All True ...

The Long Way Home

The Collected Short Stories & Other Bruises of Frank Howson

Frank Howson

Quill & Quire™
PUBLISHERS/CAPE COD

The Long Way Home

The Collected Short Stories & Bruises of Frank Howson

Quill & Quire Publishers, a Division of TreeHouse Studios, LLC
Offices 84 Court Street Plymouth, Massachusetts, USA 02360
www.quillandquirepublishing.com

Quill & Quire™
PUBLISHERS/CAPE COD

Publisher's Note: This is an autobiographical work and contains names, characters, places, and incidents are a product of the author's personal, first-hand experience. Any resemblance to actual people, living or dead, or to businesses, companies, events, institutions, or locales is often completely intentional. Get over it.

Interior Design by: Quill & Quire Publishing, a Division of TreeHouse Studios, LLC
www.quillandquirepublishing.com
Cover Design by: Barry Robinson, BR Design
Editing by: Joseph Brewer
The Long Way Home
Howson, Frank, 1952 –

Library of Congress Control Number on file.

ISBN: 978-0-692-67004-0

10 9 8 7 6 5 4 3 2 1

1. Short Stories 2. Memoir 3. Essays 4. Poetry

First Edition

Printed in the United States of America

My Thanks To ...

Henry (Jack) Francis & Pearl Howson for giving me
life and love and the freedom to be who I am.

Oliver Howson who is learning that there
are many stories but only one truth.

P.F. Sloan for his friendship, love, stories, laughs, and humanity.
The world is a colder place without you, Phil.
Barry Robinson for saving my life when I didn't think it was worth
much.
Mike Smith for his friendship, kindness and shelter from the storm.
Raija Reissenberger for her love and caring.
Warren Wills for adding the music and other vices to my life.
Phil Whelan for being my dear pal who I've somehow always
known.
Richard Wolstencroft for remembering a favour and giving me a
second chapter to my life.
J. Marshall Craig for all the fun and not-so-fun times that we both
survived together. The memory of him ordering Popeye's chicken
on Hollywood Blvd. at 3 a.m. wearing a Wookie mask will live with
me forever.
Terry Davis for the many acts of kindness and friendship
that endure in my heart.
Tommy Dysart, Joan Brockenshire & Kole Dysart for being my three
lucky charms.
Richard Morcom for always being there.
Rocky Dabscheck for his proof reading.
Theodore & Vicky Nicola for their joyful company & new ideas.
Dominic Barbuto for his friendship, loyalty, humour and kindness.
Carl Howell for his enduring friendship and shared love of music.
Bob Starkie & Christine Walters for all the laughter and good times
we have shared. May there be many more to come.
Donna Hodgson and Belinda Papal for their companionship and
caring.
Danne-Montague King & Drue Assister for their love, faith,
friendship & shelter from the storm.

Michael Snelson for always calling me "Dad."
Haven't the heart to tell him.
All the women I've met who gave me so much to write about.
Garry Spry through the ups and downs of life.
Darren G. Turner for his belief and support.
Barbara Harper for her unrelenting faith.
John & Barbara Gilbert for their friendship and belief.
John-Michael Howson and Alfie Duran for getting me back home
and adding another chapter in my life.
Ash Long and the Melbourne Observer for caring so much.
John Frost, Craig Donnell and all at JFO for giving me an audience
again.
Terry Reid & Annette Grady for all the good times.
Waddy Wachtel, Rick Rosas (RIP), Bernard Fowler, Phil Jones, Jack
Tempchin, Blondie Chaplin & Stacy Michelle for renewing my faith
in life & music.
Jonny Halliday and Oriana Wister-Zimmerman (aka Judas Priest) at
FAD Gallery.
The Hong Kong crew - Brian Greytak, Barry O'Rorke, Eric Wishart,
Neil Runcieman, Stanley Butler, Chris Exner, Kirk Kishita, Mike
Brooks, Stephen Bolton, Paul Haswell, Keith Goodman, Angus
McGowan, Jacqueline Leung, Gail Turner, Mariles Apostol, Rea de
Villena, Sandra Lam and Celina Jade. Oh, and Max and Daniel.

And so many others that they'll have to wait till the next book.

And lastly, to all those who I've met, both friend and foe alike – I
am grateful for the lessons I learned from you all.

Frank Howson

St. Kilda, 2016

I have lived a life in the circus, experiencing all the highs and lows that that brings. The tragedies only made me appreciate the good times all the more. And everything I at first thought was a curse later turned out to be a blessing. One dawn on Santa Monica Beach when I was a long way from home and had given up wanting to live, I experienced a profound moment. As I looked out at the beautiful dawning of a new morn, in that silence that is like no other, I heard a voice inside my head say, "I am not doing this to you because I hate you, but because I love you. You are a writer. I have shown you the best and the very worst of human nature. Go and write about it."

— FRANK HOWSON

CONTENTS

Forward.

By J. Marshall Craig

Anthony Newley's "What Kind of Fool Am I" blared, but it was impossible not to hear Terry Reid and Frank Howson sing over it as they danced with each other and pirouetted around the kitchen, surprisingly at the loss of not one tea cup, wine glass or tumbler of whiskey. Frank even managed a perfectly choreographed "You BASTARD!" right into the camera as I filmed the whole sordid affair. It was the 3 a.m. circus as usual when we clowns would gather … more often than not, for some strange reason, in Terry's kitchen, be that in Palm Desert or where I had first met Frank a decade earlier, in Venice, CA.

Time may have tamed each of us as our lives weave in and out because of geographical distances but our instant bond and affinity remains that of long-lost brothers no matter what the calendar pages say. When Terry introduced us, Frank and I were each deeply entrenched in our own, wildly different lives at the time. I was living near Palm Springs, brain-and soul-deep in my second, third and fourth books, while Frank, to no one's knowledge at the time, was going through some very desperate times. Unless told, no one would have known this, either, as Frank was always impeccably dressed (he used the showers at the YMCA), seemingly joyful and full of light, and made the usual rounds. We saw each other at The Joint, a Hollywood nightclub that for a magical time was famous for Monday-night jams featuring Waddy Wachtel, Rick Rosas, Phil Jones, Bernard Fowler, Terry and a who's who of rock royalty guest performers. We ran into each other predictably backstage here and there and, memorably, at a highfalutin party the Rolling Stones threw at the Four Seasons in Beverly Hills in which we had the playful joy of introducing each other to sundry rock and movies stars that he knew and I didn't, and the other way around.

Then, we lost touch. Frank returned to Australia and began, among many other things, to craft his masterful film Remembering Nigel, which life had provided him such coarse, but incalculably crucial research for, in his darkest and most desperate times in Los Angeles.

For no other reason (I thought at the time; I am now wiser to expect the not-so-random shuffling of the fate deck by the Lord) than wishing to reconnect, I found an old email for Frank and sent off a missive into the ether. He responded, despite being half a world away, within minutes, telling with excitement bordering on alarm that he was again bound for Los Angeles, had been almost desperately trying to find me, as I had moved to Santa Barbara. Two weeks later I was working on the American set of Remembering Nigel with Frank, beginning the deepest, most creative and instructive friendship a person could dream for.

Now, all these years later, comes the blessing and honor of writing the forward to Frank's first collection of short stories, essays and "other bruises," as he calls them.

I had wanted to be so clever, to prove my mettle to introduce this spectacular work of Frank's. I wrote of an American 1943 steel penny (steel as copper was diverted for the war effort) that has followed me around my whole life; I've never paid it too-close attention once learning that it's worth, well, about a penny, and as such am surprised when it just seems to turn up, every few years after a move, a massive spring cleaning or what have you. But therein is its secret, its power and the penny's true worth: Every time I find it, it reminds me of the last time I found it, and the time before and the time before … where I was, who I was with, what life I was living. I was going to fully invest myself in this metaphor of my friendship and love for Frank Howson as like this impossibly important penny that's always in my life, even if I don't see it every day. It can't be put on a pedestal or framed, caged or controlled, as it asks nothing of me but to be left to work its magic in its own way. A truffle pig of a penny…

But metaphors won't stick to a singularly original man such as Frank Howson. I can't put him on a pedestal, and would never wish to frame him (though many have tried, and failed), cage him or anything else. No, what I am able to do, instead of the usual note of thanks or praise or suggestion to the reader, is to say with certain authority that every word Frank writes comes from him having lived it. He's a man who takes notes, which, for a man with a photographic memory, is a powerful thing. Thank God he uses it for good. Enjoy, and soak up these life lessons for which Frank has paid so dearly, and for which we get for the humble cost of a book.

J. Marshall

Cape Cod, 2016

Part One: The Short Stories

{ 1 }

Jake Everson's Death

J ake Everson woke up one day in New Orleans and
picked up the newspaper to discover he'd died the
previous morning in Spain.

He froze. Suddenly the beautiful sunlight and noise
of the street melted away. He studied the photograph
they'd used of him – one when he was young and
starting out – his eyes burning with ambition. Yes, it was

him alright. He even remembered the photo-shoot and the female photographer he'd gone on to marry and disappoint. He'd adored women but had never found the right one, and now accepted the fact that he'd probably always be alone.

His hands started trembling uncontrollably and the paper fell from them. He ran to the mirror and took a good long look at himself. He had lately avoided his reflection as he was having difficulty accepting himself as an older man. But there he was. Anxiety sweat forming on his brow and his lined face contorted and tense with the shock of his reported demise. A million thoughts stampeded through his head but all of them were rushing by too fast to grab a hold of. He looked down at the empty scotch glass from the night before and picked it up. He could see his distorted reflection in the bottom of it and his hand tightened with a mixture of panic and confusion, causing it to crack and smash, filling his palm with the fragments of splintered glass.

He opened his hand and saw he was bleeding. He studied this with the detached observation of someone numb with fear. He looked up at himself in the mirror again and wondered who had played this sick joke on him. Whoever it was he or she would pay. He was still a man with power. He could get things done. His name still meant something and in some circles so did he. No, he was not dead. He laughed at the absurdity of it all. Sure, his career had died many times in the past but he'd somehow been able to keep coming back. A book here, a magazine article there. But, this was different, it was there in the newspaper. This said he was really dead. Finito. Gone.

Didn't Will Rogers once say that the only thing he believed was what he read in the newspapers? Now, poor old Will seemed so out of touch with the current state of journalism. This was the era where they can say anything they want about you and mostly get away with it. Jake had for years sadly lamented the demise of objective reporting. Will Rogers lived in a different world. A world where they reported the facts and left the reader to draw their own conclusions. These days Jake could tell a reporter's political leanings one paragraph into a news story. He also remembered the famous William Boyd case where a newspaper reported that Boyd had been charged with murder and printed a photograph of the actor William Boyd, our beloved Hopalong Cassidy. Trouble was, it was the wrong William Boyd and killed Hoppy's career for many years.

Well Jake wasn't going to take it. He was going to go down swinging. He'd have his lawyers all over them tomorrow, extracting a huge settlement and an apology. Yeah. It turned him on to be so forceful. He rushed back to the bed, knocking over something in his trail without stopping to see what, and sat to re-read the article. Yep, he was dead alright. Well, as far as the press were concerned. This had to be worth millions. With a morbid fascination he read quotes from his friends and enemies alike. Now, for once, they all seemed to agree that he was a great guy and an important writer. Jake smiled. One of those smiles you give when you are engulfed by anger and feel you can just smile it away. It was a joke, surely? That's it. A sick joke. He checked the date at the top of the page to see if it was April First. But, no, it was still March. He got an idea. He phoned the hotel operator.

"Yes Mr. Everson?"

"Ex-excuse me, but can you h-h-hear me?" stammered Jake.

"Yes of course, sir."

"How do I sound?"

"Are you unwell, Mr. Everson? I can send a doctor to your room?"

"No … no … I'm okay. That's right, I'm okay. I feel good in fact."

Do you wish to be put through to room service, Mr. Everson?"

Why not, thought Jake. I mean, if I'm dead I can't be responsible for my debts right? He laughed. His humor had always gotten him through dire situations in the past. He was witty. His glib lines were famous amongst his associates. He'd joked his way through three divorces and countless lovers. Jake spoke to room service and ordered two lobsters and a bottle of French champagne. Oh, and some caviar. Lots of caviar. "It's fun being dead," he wise-cracked to himself, enjoying the joke. He'd treat himself to a feast worthy of a king, and while savouring it he'd plot the demise of the asshole who'd planted this bullshit in the press.

"Oh yes!" he muttered out loud, "That hack will wish he was dead when my lawyer gets through with him!"

Jake was good at revenge. Sometimes he'd held grudges for years. Sometimes those grudges got him through his life – hanging on, driven by the urge to have the last laugh. Then a new dread set in. His son Oliver would read this and think he'd be all alone in the world now. Jake speed dialed his son but it rang out and went to the message bank. This was all he got these days. First the public had lost interest in him. Then the publishers. Now his son.

"Oliver, this is your Dad. Just wanted to say don't read the newspaper. It's full of crap. Your father's not dead. In fact, I've never felt better. Whoever is responsible for this will pay, so help me God. By the time Brent, Cowan, Zachman, and Garber get through with him I'll own the newspaper! Anyway, hope you're well son … and having a good time. I love you. Bye … Oh, call me sometime."

Jake hung up and kicked the bedside table. He was seething with rage. This is not the way things were in all the stories he'd written. He'd always tied things up. Clarified. Resolved loose ends. A final paragraph filled with hope, new beginnings. Now he realized why he'd become a writer in the first place. He had control over life in his stories. He was God. Well, actually a kinder, more caring God than the real guy. Everything made sense. Everything added up to something. Maybe that's why they call it fiction. He frantically dialed his agent's number.

"Hello Marie? Can you hear me?"

"Yes, Mr. Everson. Would you like to be put through to Mr. Craig?"

Jake sighed, relieved,

"Yes put me through to Jeff please."

He waited for what seemed an eternity. His agent was probably schmoozing some new hip writer.

"Hello, Jake?" answered Jeff in an upbeat, friendly voice.

"Jeff, am I dead?"

"No, Jake, the reviews have been mostly positive."

"I mean, really dead? I just read about my death in the morning paper. They even quoted you saying what a tragedy this was for the literary world. Listen, Jeff, if this is some practical joke or a sick publicity stunt to boost sales, I am going to fucking kill someone, got it? I'm Jake Everson! It's not over till I say it is, alright? Alright?!"

Jake realized he was screaming. There was a silence. Then, in a tone he'd come to know so well, "Jake, are you okay? Have you been drinking again?"

"No, not a drop since January. But it's things like this that remind me why I drank. You need to get onto this newspaper publisher and read them the riot act. I want a retraction. I want an apology. I want compensation! Hear me?!

"But …" attempted Jeff.

"But fucking nothing! For the first time in your life will you actually do what I tell you?" hissed Jake.

There was a deathly silence now. Jake took a deep breath and tried to find a more reasonable pitch, "Listen, Jeffrey, I read the morning paper here and there's a whole article in it about my … death."

Jeff laughed, "It must be another Jake Everson."

The air that rushed through Jake's mouth and into the receiver convinced Jeff to change tact.

"Okay, okay, Jake … fine. But I need you to calm down. Let me call them and get to the bottom of it. It's probably another person with the same name and they've done a William Boyd with it. Did I ever tell you the William Boyd story?"

"About two hundred times," sighed Jake, suddenly feeling weary from the energy he'd dissipated, "They printed my photo, they mentioned my books, my friends, my marriages, the whole shebang."

"What?! I haven't spoken to any reporters about you. This is bullshit!"

Now Jeff was pissed, "Jake, you are not dead. You are speaking to me on the phone, alright? There's obviously been some mistake and I'll get right onto it. Trust me, I'm going to rip 'em a new asshole!"

"It says I died in Spain."

Jeff then took on the tone of someone speaking to a child, "Jake, where are you?"

"New Orleans."

"Alright then. New Orleans is not Spain. And it's a fucking long way from Heaven, trust me."

Jake closed his eyes as tears of relief welled up. He felt stupid about getting so worked up over this. What a fool he must sound like.

"Jake, have the front desk fax me a copy of the article and I'll get right onto it."

"Thanks, Jeff ... sorry ... I feel like an idiot but..."

"Don't worry about it, my friend. As soon as I have the article I'll phone the editor and he'll be the one wishing he was dead!"

"Thanks."

Jake loved it when Jeff talked tough. He'd had so few people in his life stand up for him. Jake hung up. He ripped the article out of the paper, stuffed some money into a pocket, and rushed down the stairs, not even waiting for the elevator. He told the guy at the front desk to fax it immediately and gave him Jeff's number as well as a twenty-dollar bill for his trouble.

"Yes, Mr. Everson, I'll fax it straight away."

Then Jake turned towards the open doors. There was some kind of parade going on outside.

Ah, that's right. It was Mardi Gras time in the Big Easy. The sound and movement of life. He found himself gravitating towards it. Next thing he was out on the pavement as clowns, men on stilts, beauty queens, brass bands and drunken freaks wearing masks passed him by.

He pushed his way through the crowd but no one noticed him, there was too much else going on. He felt strange. As though he was looking at Life for the first time. He stared at people and noticed things that normally his busy schedule would have blurred. Most passers-by thought he was just another drunk. One alcoholic even wanted to fight him for some reason that only seems logical after a bottle of cheap scotch. Jake laughed uncontrollably. What did it matter if someone struck him? It felt good to still be here.

He wasn't sure how long he stood there, a man in the way, amidst the sea of moving bodies. It was as though time had stood still. Maybe five minutes passed, maybe an hour. He didn't care, he had plenty of time to kill. This explained why he wasn't at the hotel when Jeff phoned to ask why he'd faxed an article about trout fishing.

Jake saw a boy with a kite looking skyward and laughing. The kid then let go and watched his kite fly towards the heavens, swooping and soaring like an eagle.

A homeless man asked for some change and Jake, uncharacteristically, took the time to actually look into the poor unfortunate's eyes and acknowledge his existence. He even asked the man his name before emptying his pockets to him.

He passed a gypsy lady reading tarot cards and she screamed something at him but it sounded like a trombone and merged with the deafening passing cacophony. Jake realized he was still in his pajamas but it was okay.

No one noticed.

No one cared.

He looked down at his bare feet, now dirty from the street, and thought about his mother for the first time in years. Oh, how he suddenly missed her. A tear came to his eye and he wanted her to find him and hold him to her breast and whisper in his ear, "Now, now, Jakey, it's alright … it's alright."

Her little boy was lost. That's all. But his mother was lost too. Taken by an unfeeling God who played with us like we were pawns in some bizarre game only He could make sense of. Did it give the Almighty pleasure to take a young mother from her little boy? If so, Jake hated Him. Come to think of it, he hated so many. Most of all he hated what didn't make sense.

He made it through the moving throng and found himself in the middle of the road in some side street. He saw a beautiful woman on the corner. She looked like an angel, young, brunette, exquisite features. The kind of girl he always lost his heart to in the days when he was young and had dreams.

"Hello!" he yelled.

She turned and fixed him with those dark, mysterious eyes. She yelled something back but her voice was drowned out by the brass bands and party atmosphere of the celebrations.

He couldn't hear her. Nor the siren of the approaching fire-truck. She was the last thing he saw before the blinding light.

He drifted, as he had done most of his life, towards this light. Yes, he guessed he was really dead now. Holy fuck. This is more like he imagined it would be. It made more sense. He looked back down and saw what remained of a body. Momentarily he didn't even recognize it was him. How could it be? This man seemed older than his years, and weary. How embarrassing, his bald spot was totally exposed and people were gathering. His once youthful handsome face had, in recent years, been replaced by a bitter, defeated look. That look you get from too many "no thank yous." It pained him to see himself with such clarity. He turned away and looked up as his eyes adjusted to the light and his body felt a warmth that can only be explained as having a warm bath internally.

When he was finally totally engulfed by what appeared to be a white room he stopped floating, and a dark figure made his way to him. A man in a black bowler hat and a dark suit, or so it seemed. He shook Jake's hand in the manner of a bank manager greeting a new customer.

"It's alright, Mr. Everson, we've been expecting you. Sorry for the theatrics but we needed to get you out of your damn room so you could make our appointment. What you saw was a copy of tomorrow's paper. You were very well loved y'know? – and will be sorely missed. But I guess you already know that now, huh?"

"But the newspaper said I died in Spain?"

"No, that was a typo. The editor was still hung-over from the festivities. There'll be a correction in the later editions."

"What about my son?"

"Don't worry, he'll be fine. He grows up to be a very successful writer. Even more so than you."

"Where is God? I have a few things I want to tell him!" hissed Jake.

The man in the bowler hat smiled, "Most people do. He's heard it all before y'know but, if it helps you, by all means get it off your chest."

Jake continued walking with this stranger towards the light and with each step seemed to feel more relaxed and accepting of his fate. All the anger and regret of his life fell away step by step.

He was almost there when suddenly he thought about the lobster, champagne and caviar waiting in his room. He laughed uncontrollably again. The kind of convulsive laughter you don't think will ever stop. He thought to himself that it was so typical of his life, and wished he could write about it. He then found his laughter had turned to sobbing. A bittersweet sobbing. He felt so alone. Why did he always end up alone?

Just then he heard his mother's voice, "Now, now, Jakey ... it's alright ... it's alright. I've been waiting for you. You never have to be alone again." And with that, she took his hand and together they walked.

Just like old times.

FRANK HOWSON

{ 2 }

The Birthday Boy

T he old man had clearly lost his mind. The young
nurses at the home all loved him. He made them
laugh. He regaled them with stories of his youth
and all the beautiful women he'd known who'd loved
him too.

These days his mind wandered and he found it increasingly difficult to concentrate for too long on any one subject or thought or conversation. But he always had a smile for you. His Mum had taught him that. "It doesn't cost anything y'know and it can brighten up someone's life." He'd taken her advice seriously, as he'd done with most things she'd said, and he became known as a smiler. No matter how disastrous the turns of his life were he had a smile for you. Maybe that's why he'd been taken into the hearts of so many lovely women who'd enjoyed his company.

He couldn't much tell what was a memory or what was a dream anymore. Perhaps at some point it doesn't really matter.

He wondered whether he'd told the nurses about how Marilyn Monroe had once stopped on the street to return his smile and touch his cheek. He could still feel her warm hand when he closed his eyes. She was so much softer in real life, and had the most beautiful caring eyes. He couldn't help but tell her how much he loved her and she just smiled at him, the way Goddesses do. It was a sympathetic smile to one who could never have her in a million years but because of her soft heart she cared enough to leave him this beautiful memory. Something she knew would one day keep an old man warm.

He remembered being a young child and seeing the great Australian boxer Les Darcy step out of the shadows of a doorway and smile at him. Les was confident and successful and even a kid knew he was bound for glory. And then he was gone. He would die at 21, lost and despairing, so far from home. "Why did God take such a perfect specimen from this world and leave me?" thought the old man. What have I ever contributed to the world other than a smile? Yet those I have met were great. Truly great. They touched people's lives and then like a comet were gone in a blast of dazzling fire.

"Hello, Mr. Cuthbertson, do you want the chicken noodle or the vegetable soup today?" asked the young nurse Rochelle.

The old man looked up at her beautiful young face and couldn't help but smile.

"Has anybody ever told you how beautiful you are?" he asked.

She laughed. "Yes, Mr. Cuthbertson, you do every day. Now is it chicken noodle or vegetable?"

"I don't care, love, it's all shit."

He fought the urge to tell her he hoped she'd never get to this stage. It would sound inappropriate to wish an early death on someone so sweet. And she wouldn't understand.

"Okay, I'll get you the vegetable. It'll be good for you. We need you to stay around, don't we?"

Why? he thought.

He looked at her beautiful curves as she walked away from him and smiled at how years ago he would've been beside himself with lust. Now, he could just appreciate the curves for what they were. Like admiring a masterpiece of art. Life does become simpler the closer you get to night. All the bullshit stuff just dies away and leaves you with the heart of things.

He looked out the window and watched the children in a nearby school playing. He remembered how he used to play with a young girl named Enid who lived in his street. They used to make mud pies and play house. These games were all Enid's idea and he didn't much like them but he pretended to and played them out of his great love for her. She told him she would marry him when they were older and that they'd never be apart. But then his parents moved to another house and Enid must've found it too far to travel. Or perhaps her parents couldn't be bothered dropping her off. He often wondered what had happened to Enid. He hoped she'd had a good life and hadn't wasted it waiting for him. He had a strong sense of responsibility and hated letting anyone down. If he saw her today he'd give her his best smile. All the girls had liked his smile. He had some teeth missing now. Poverty had set in and it was impossible on his budget to replace them. Or anything really. It made him feel self-conscious. But he smiled anyway because it was all he knew how to do and too hard a habit to break. Besides, most times people smiled back and that gave him such a warm feeling inside.

"Having a good smile can open doors, son." Yes, Mum, I've never forgotten. "Good boy."

He thought again about all the lovely women that'd been in his life and was confused and sometimes angry that he hadn't been able to keep any of them. Some had lasted years, but every time the money ran out, so did they. He had learnt that poverty takes away so much. It is certainly very hard on a relationship. Yes, a smile may open doors, but money closes them.

Back in his mind he thought about the night he had met Sophia Loren in Los Angeles. He happened to be at a hotel and she was dining there with some girlfriends. She was so taken with him that she called him over. He sat by her side and gave her his smile and she smiled back.

"I like you" she said, "You have a very kind face."

Then she took his hand and they chatted. All night people came over and praised her. At the end of the evening he asked her if she ever got bored with being adored.

She smiled and said, "Yes. Sometimes I do."

She held his gaze and they looked into each other's eyes for a long time. It was a perfect moment and perhaps he could've died there and then as life wouldn't get much better. But he didn't know that, yet. When she was leaving he took her hand and kissed it.

She said, "I love you, you are such a gentleman. Your mother taught you manners."

He gave her another of his smiles and knew somewhere in the other world his mother was smiling too. She walked out of the hotel and he went to the men's room.

Upon his return he saw that she was still lingering at the front door and looking in his direction. He froze, realizing that she must want more. In shock, nervous and not prepared for this, he foolishly walked on back to the lounge and to a life of regretting his cowardice.

But maybe it was better this way. He still had the golden untarnished dream of a perfect night and the sweet painful bliss of unrequited love. What if she'd tired of his smile. And then him. As so many had done. This way she lives on in the heart.

"Here you are, Mr. Cuthbertson, your lovely freshly made vegetable soup."

He looked up and smiled at her and said, "Thank you."

She smiled back. "You have such lovely manners, Mr. Cuthbertson. Did anyone ever tell you that?"

He smiled again as tears welled in his eyes, "Yes, someone once did. A long time ago."

The next morning, Nurse Rochelle reported to duty. One of the other nurses rushed to her. "Did you hear about Mr. Cuthbertson?"

"No?"

"He died a few hours ago."

"Oh no, I loved that man."

"We all did. We've been trying to locate family but not sure he has any. Well, none still living. He was calling out the name "Enid" and seemed to be upset about not saying goodbye to her. Do you know anything about her? Or how we could contact her?"

"No, I've never heard of her."

"He also mentioned Sophia Loren."

For a moment they both laughed through their tears. "But I think that may have been one of his dreams."

But Nurse Rochelle wasn't so sure. "You never know. He had such a lovely smile. I bet we'd be surprised who that man had met."

They both stood there for some time not quite sure what else they could say. But knowing that their lives were now in some way inexplicably diminished by the man who had lived in Room 142.

"Oh shit," said Nurse Rochelle.

"What?" asked the Nurse Bothemly.

"Today was his birthday. I'd organized a cake for him."

"Well, let's have it, and a glass of cheap champagne and watch a Sophia Loren movie. Do you think he really knew Ms. Loren?"

"I hope he did. And I hope she loved him." They laughed. Then cried again.

{ 3 }

The Icon

R obert Travell was about to make a comeback. It seemed like all anyone had talked about for the past few months, the return of the '60s music icon whose songs helped changed the world and stop a war. You couldn't turn on the TV, radio, pick up a newspaper or surf the Internet without seeing the excited commotion this had caused. It was rumored that

Columbia Records were paying him a million-dollar advance for his first album in 30 years.

What had happened to him? At the height of his career he just disappeared. Retired. Became a recluse. Periodically there were sightings of him – or someone resembling him – in diners, at bus depots, on a construction site, but nothing ever confirmed. Some say he'd gone mad like Howard Hughes and now had a beard to his knees – others say he did a J.D. Salinger and had simply had enough of the prying eye of the press and public and was now working as a history teacher in some rural area school. The truth is, no one knew.

The magazine I worked for had assigned me to interview the great man on this eve of his return. I was only 21 at the time and had missed Mr. Travell's glory years, but had grown up in a home where my parents had played his records ad-infinitum. In many ways he felt like a member of my family. Like a beloved uncle I was yet to meet.

I was given his address and the appointed time for the interview. The address was in a little street in West Hollywood. It seemed an odd location for him as I knew the street well and the homes and apartments there were all very modest. I would've expected a mansion befitting this man's contribution to the world, but I was young and yet to learn about the music business and the thieves that run it.

On the day that I almost had a car accident because I was so tense and my mind was on everything other than the road. I pulled up outside the address and had to recheck it as I couldn't believe this little house in disrepair could possibly be where the great Robert Travell had ended up.

I knocked on the door. There was no answer. My disappointment went straight to my stomach and I felt sick. I must've written down the wrong address. Maybe I misheard the interview time. Oh shit. I'd been given the chance to interview Robert Travell and I'd screwed it up. Just as I was beating myself up on the porch, I heard a voice.

"I'm around the back! Come to the backyard."

Oh thank God! He's home. Well, around the back. I then began the grand adventure to get to the back yard. I had to maneuver my way past several rusted out cars, knee-high grass, an old discarded washing machine, and through garments that looked like they'd been hanging on the clothes-line for several years. Finally, after some time, I succeeded in reaching the backyard but no one was there. Then, from inside I heard, "Where are you?"

I now realized he'd gone to the front door in search of me. My fantasized wonderful interview with the great man was rapidly descending into a farce.

"I'm here!" I yelled out but doubted if he could hear me.

I opened the back door and walked in. I could see him, his back to me, at the front door. I was silenced by awe and fear. I heard him grumble something to himself and then he closed the door and turned. Lost in his thoughts he was almost up to me before he saw me. He stopped with a jolt.

"Who are you? And what are you doing in my house?"

This was now a Laurel and Hardy sketch and I just wanted to turn and run from the embarrassment.

"Ahhh, I'm Suzie Montrose. I'm here to interview you, Mr. Travell. I'm sorry, I went to the backyard and you weren't there so I just came in. I'm so sorry. I'm usually very well mannered."

He smiled and his whole face softened. "You are well-mannered, Suzie. I see that in your eyes. A cup of green tea, perhaps?"

"Yes. Oh thank you, Mr. Travell, thank you so much. That would be lovely." I hate green tea but at this moment I was so looking forward to it.

As Mr. Travell walked into the kitchen to prepare the tea, which he did with great care as though it was a sacred ritual, I studied his living room for clues about him. I looked at his book shelf which usually revealed a lot about a person. But in this case it was empty except for one book – "The Art of Dentistry."

"Mr. Travell. I see you're interested in dentistry" I yelled out so he could hear me in the kitchen.

"No, not at all. A friend of mine gave that to me."

"Your dentist?"

"No, he's a carpenter."

This man was becoming more and more fascinating and enigmatic by the second. How could someone so great with words be the owner of only one book?

He suddenly appeared with a tray and our teas. He took great care to place my cup on the coffee table in front of me. I could see his hands shook a little. Perhaps he'd been an alcoholic? Or maybe by caring too much as illustrated in all his songs he'd burnt out his nervous system.

"Don't you read many books, Mr. Travell?"

"No. I find they contain too many words."

He sat. "Never read a book that couldn't be improved by cutting it in half."

I wasn't sure whether he was serious or just having me on. I was lost for words so he jumped back in to fill up the void.

41

"For instance, "A Tale of Two Cities" would've been much better, in my opinion, as a tale of one city. But what do I know?" Then he smiled.

I was speechless and had nothing to add to that, so I drank my green tea. All of it, in order to buy some time to think.

"Ah, we're off to a great start! I see we have something in common."

"Huh? What's that?" I asked.

"A love of green tea."

"Oh yes, I can't get enough of it," I lied.

"Well I shall get you some more."

And so he did, and poured it slowly and with considerable care.

Desperate to say something to fill out the silence, I uttered, "I see you live very simply, Mr. Travell."

"Two divorces and a record company that robbed me blind. I have always admired Jesse James. At least he was honest about what he was."

"You must be excited about your new album?" I ventured on.

"No."

"But the whole world is waiting for it."

"Are they really? Isn't that sad?"

I had nowhere to go with this interview and was losing any grasp I had on an angle for the story.

He looked at me for a long time. I was used to that, being a woman and interviewing sleazy rock stars. But Travell's look was different. He was looking at me – into me – as though seeing my soul. There was nothing sexual about it. His caring eyes exuded the warmth of a father. For the first time in my life I felt safe. And loved.

"Here's the deal. Forget this interview, I know how they go, you ask the standard questions and I give you the standard answers. Why don't you hang out with me for the rest of this week and get to know me. The real me. Y'see everyone I've ever met has written a book about me, as well as all the people I never met. They all seem to be an expert on my life. And y'know something? It's all bullshit and lies. And seeing this will be my last foray into the public, why don't you take the time to get me right?"

"Really? How do you know you can trust me?" I asked.

He smiled again, "I can trust you. You have a shining soul. You must protect that, but I'll tell you how to do that later in the week. Now, who's for some doughnuts? I know a wonderful place and it's so much superior to those Krispy Krap ones."

I loved this man already. "Yes, count me in!"

And so off we went on another adventure. This is how the whole week was. A series of adventures with a man who, if he was mad, it was a madness like Don Quixote – a madness that cut through all the ugliness of the world and taught you that there was love in everything. If you looked hard enough.

That week I had the best doughnuts ever. We also went to a baseball game; sat on Venice Beach and saw and heard the drum ceremony at sunset; ate in diners and all the while talked about our lives. He asked me why I was working for a stupid magazine that only interviewed stupid celebrities. I told him my dream was to buy my own little apartment so I'd never have to struggle to pay rent again. He told me I could achieve that without selling my soul.

I was concerned for him because he fell several times that week. Literally. He had so much pride he was back on his feet within seconds. He told me he had dizzy spells occasionally and was on medication for it. In fact, he seemed to be on a lot of medication. He had pills in every pocket and regularly took them.

Every time I asked him about his new album he changed the subject. All he would confirm was that it was finished. And so was he. It would be the last.

"So that means it must contain some interesting statements about the present day and age?" I ventured.

"You could say that," he smiled mischievously.

"Why did you walk away for so long?"

"I didn't walk; I was driven away actually. But that's a story of greed and darkness and why ruin our meal? Anyway, I'd said everything I wanted to say in all those songs. Each one of them deals with a different aspect of life and, seeing the world unfortunately hasn't changed, I have nothing new to add. To have gone on would've meant I'd have just been repeating myself, which so many artists do. You have to have the class to know when to go. You owe it to the public to leave their fantasy about you untarnished."

"So, with the new album – are you taking music in a new direction?" I bravely asked.

He looked momentarily disappointed in me. But then the warm smile returned. "I am giving the music industry what it deserves."

He then looked sad, and turned away indicating he'd said all he was going to say about that.

I asked him if he had any children.

"Yes. But they were taken away from me years ago by mothers who convinced them I was mad and dangerous to be with. Not a day goes by that my heart doesn't break when I think of them. I hope they have grown to be good people and that they are safe."

That night we walked back to his place. When we got there he was genuinely concerned about me driving home.

"I won't hear of it. You've had three glasses of wine over dinner and that's enough to get you in trouble with the cops or worse still be involved in an accident. You can sleep in my bed; I'll sleep on the couch."

"No, no, I'll sleep on the couch."

"Nope, that's the deal. Besides, I like the couch. It's my friend. To tell you the truth I fall asleep here most nights."

Then he looked at me and said, "You are safe here you know?"

"I know that. In fact, I have never felt safer." I am so glad I said that to him.

The next morning, I got up and went out into the living room. He was sitting up asleep, or so I thought. After some time, I touched him and he was stone cold. As cold as a statue. As cold as the monument they would eventually erect of him. I ran screaming into the street. I wanted to tell the world he was gone. I wanted to tell them everything was now changed. A light had gone out. He was no more.

I watched them take away his body. But that was not him. It was just a body. I lied and said I was his daughter just so I could sit in his house and feel his spirit a bit longer. On his table I found a CD that had scribbled on it "The New Album." With trembling hands, I put it on and sat on his friendly couch to listen to Robert Travell's last statement to the world.

The first track was Robert reciting "Mary Had A Little Lamb." The second track was a diatribe about what thieves record companies are.

And so it went on. Ten tracks in all. He had delivered ten tracks and fulfilled his contractual obligations, and thus could keep his million-dollar advance.

I started to laugh, uncontrollably. This was his "fuck you" to a record industry that had fucked him long and hard. The record company would later issue a statement saying that the reason the album wouldn't be released was due to the fact that it was unfinished and in respect of Mr. Travell's important legacy they would shelve it.

In his will he left each of his two children $400,000 plus all the royalties from his record and publishing catalogues. And to me he left $200,000 so that I would never have to struggle to pay rent again.

I have quit my job writing about other people's lives and have started a Robert Travell Charity Foundation to help homeless people. I am also writing my first book and making sure it's not too long.

Every night I sit on the couch, his couch, in my apartment, sip my green tea and give thanks that he came along and that I was lucky enough to know him. Really know him. Trouble is, I fear he has ruined me for any other man. You see, a Robert Travell comes along just once in a lifetime. If you're lucky. Although I live in hope that I will find his spirit in someone else. And that that someone will look into my eyes and really see me. And I will feel loved and safe again.

Recently I was offered a million dollars to write about my experiences with him. I told them to go fuck themselves. And somewhere, Robert Travell laughed, and I was filled with a warmth deep inside. A warmth that told me he was proud of me and that I'd turned out alright. In his words, I'd grown to be a "good person."

Dinner At 8

I t was one of those lovely old houses that had once been resplendent but, like most of us, had fallen on harder times. Still, it bravely hung onto its former dignity. So well in fact that it was not uncommon for people to stop and look up at it with some admiration. Perhaps trying to imagine it in its glory years. The era of parties and money, before a few wars gave the world a reality shock.

I was moving in to this huge old monolith. A friend of mine had recommended that I contact the owner, Mr. Roger Thesbold, when he knew I was searching for something. My friend thought it would suit me. "It has style and personality, and isn't that old looking if you don't look too close," he'd wisecracked.

So here I was, moving the last of my boxes into a place I thought may be home for a while. I'd been looking for home for some time. Maybe most of my life. I'd come close to having a home on a few occasions but lost them in the settlement with two wives whose lawyers felt their clients were more at home in them than I was. I couldn't argue with them. I'm not sure I've ever felt at home, anywhere. But I was an eternal optimist and maybe this would be the place where I'd live out my last chapter.

Roger Thesbold was there to greet me. He was dressed in a suit, shirt and tie even though it was a Saturday morning. And yet he looked relaxed in it as though he was wearing jeans and a T-shirt. I guess he'd dressed that way for so long it felt natural to him. I, on the other hand, was dressed for carrying boxes and I hoped my attire and body odor didn't offend this delicate refined man too much.

"Hello Roger!" I called out to him and gave an enthusiastic wave. I was still having trouble calling him Roger. He was so dignified it almost felt like I should be addressing him as Lord Thesbold.

Lord Thesbold didn't help with the carrying of the boxes. That would've been beneath him. I doubt if he'd ever picked up anything heavier than a butter knife or a book of English verse. But here we were, two unlikely house mates determined to give it our best shot.

By the time I had emptied the last boxes and found a place for them in my bedroom, it was approximately 4 p.m.

I thought I heard Roger chatting to someone. Perhaps there'd been a delivery or maybe a guest had dropped in. I hadn't heard the door bell but I may've been preoccupied. I put my ear against the door and there it was. The sound of two men chatting. One voice was that of Roger's and the other I didn't recognize. He sounded old. Very old. I finished hanging clothes in the wardrobe, as well as finding places for my knick knacks and mementoes, and then decided to have a quick shower and change into clean clothes to prepare for dinner.

About an hour later I walked into the living room and found Roger having a scotch on ice. He immediately jumped to his feet and offered me one. I liked the old world feeling of this place and the almost creepy old world manners of my host.

"This scotch is over a hundred years old, Mr. Mulliner."

"Oh please, call me David," I replied, then added, "I hope it's not wasted on me I'm not really a scotch connoisseur. Never had the budget for it."

"Taste it," said Roger.

I did, and tried hard to pull a face that said all the things he wanted to hear.

"Oh my, yes, it is very good isn't it? Marvelous!" I don't know why I used the word "marvelous" as I hadn't for many years but there was something about Roger and his world that made it totally appropriate. He smiled and told me to sit. Like a well trained puppy, I did.

"Well David, how are you settling in?" he asked.
"Fine, Roger. It's looking like home already," I lied.

"Splendid indeed. That is what we want to hear. I usually dine about 8 p.m. I hope that's not too late for you. You know, old traditions die hard."
"No, not at all," again I lied. In fact, I was so hungry I thought I may be ready to eat one of his Persian rugs by 8 p.m.

Then there was a lull in the conversation. I scanned the huge bookshelves of hard cover books, no doubt first editions, and was impressed. There was something comforting about books. Having given so much of your time to them and taken so much knowledge from them, I guess they became like old friends and it was nice to be able to have them join us. Suddenly I wished one of those brilliant authors would say something because I'd gone dry.

"Oh, another scotch!" said Roger, leaping to his feet. Within seconds he'd taken my glass and strode to the very well stocked bar to pour another aged scotch that would be utterly wasted on me.

Searching for something to say, I grasped at the only thing I could think of, "You had a guest before?"

Roger stopped and almost dropped the precious bottle.

What do you mean?"

He turned and looked at me, a startled look on his face.

"Before. I heard you talking to someone. An older man."

"You must be hearing things. Perhaps it was the television," he spluttered.

I looked around the room and noticed there was no television. Certainly not in this room.

"But I recognized your voice. And you were talking to someone," I pushed on.

"I'm afraid not. As I said, you must be hearing things."

Roger crossed the room and handed me my glass replenished with old man's scotch and ice. He then sat down and stared into the bottom of his glass for some time.

"I'm sorry if I've upset you," I volunteered.

"No. Not all. It's this house. A lot of things have happened in this house, especially this room. And sometimes people don't understand. It's for those reasons that I never ever entertained the idea of a house guest. But Mr. Braff knew it was time."

"Who's Mr. Braff?" I asked.

"Mr. Henry Braff. He's the real owner of this house."

"I thought he was dead. I read about the history of this place and I'm sure it stated the original owner died in the 1950s. I may be wrong, of course." I decided to shut up.

Roger slowly lifted his head and turned to look at me. He had a strange expression. Otherworldly. An expression that was so calm it unnerved you.

"Do you believe in the afterlife, David?"

I didn't know quite how to respond to this. Especially when every cell in me wanted to run to the front door, down the steps and never be seen again. But I was a man and we're not supposed to act like that. "I don't know what I believe, Roger. Do you?"

Roger smiled and my heart skipped a beat. "Oh yes, I believe. Mr. Braff is with us now. He likes you. He likes you a lot. Don't you, Mr. Braff?"

Then Roger turned his head and looked at the empty couch next to me. But I could tell from his expression he was convinced he was seeing someone. I have no doubt he could see Mr. Henry Braff. No doubt at all. I looked down into my scotch and watched the ice slowly melting away. I felt it was the safest place to look. At least there I had something to hold onto. And then I heard and recognized the old man's voice from some hours before.

"Hello David, I'm Henry Braff. It's a great pleasure to finally see you again. This house has been awaiting your return for a very long time. So have I."

I was so terrified; I didn't want to look to my left. For if I saw the image of Henry Braff I was convinced I would have a heart attack on the spot and drop dead away.

I looked down at my hands holding the glass of scotch and they were trembling like I was having a convulsion. Some of the scotch was actually shaken from the glass and spilt over the sides onto the expensive rug.

I slowly turned my head, for no other reason than I must know, and there was an old, old man sitting but a few feet away from me. Although I wanted to die to end the confusion in my mind, I was compelled to keep looking at him.

He was smiling. It was a kind smile. A smile that made me feel that I was safe. "You have had a hard life haven't you, David?"

I didn't know what to say. I'd never thought of my life that way. I'd just always gotten up from the floor every time I'd been knocked down, and went on. No questions asked. No self pity. It was what a man did wasn't it?

"Your hardship was so unnecessary. In fact, it was all because your mother wanted to hurt me. And that she did. She even changed her name so that I could not find her. But in her thirst for revenge she hurt herself and you very badly. Altered your lives. It took her to an early grave, and it cursed you to a life of wandering and never finding a home."

I felt a tear fall down my cheek and suddenly I was a man no more, but a little boy lost and confused.

"I'm your grandfather, David. And I have waited so long to have you here. Now I can rest in peace knowing you are at last safe. Roger is in charge of a trust fund that was set aside for you a long time ago. You will never need to worry about money again nor a roof over your head. All I ask is that Roger continues to live here too in reward for all his loyalty to me … and now to you."

"I don't know what to say."

Henry Braff smiled, "I had waited most of my life for this moment but unfortunately I was called away some years ago. God has granted me this opportunity to come back and talk to you. Don't fret. Your mother and I have resolved everything and she is with me."

"With you?"

"Yes. We may drop in from time to time to see you, if that won't unnerve you too much?"

"You … and my mother? No, no not all."

"Well now, it's dinner time," said Roger.

"How can dinner be ready? We've been too busy talking?" said I.

Henry Braff smiled again. "Well you're in for a treat, my boy. Remember how good a cook your mother was and all those meals she made for you? And how you always asked her for seconds and then thirds and told her she was the greatest cook ever? You even told two of your wives that, which they didn't appreciate that much but I guess you realize that now."

Then I heard a voice. The voice. It was a sound I hadn't heard since I was a boy and yet it was so a part of me that it filled me and made me whole again. I then turned to see my mother. She hadn't aged and was still as beautiful as I remembered. She smiled at me with tears in her eyes and said, "I'm so sorry."

I stood out of respect for her, "Sorry for what?"

"Sorry for the hardship you suffered because of my stubbornness. Sorry for not being here to comfort you. Sorry for a life you didn't deserve."

"There is nothing to be forgiven or to be sorry about. Everything I went through made me better. Every fall taught me humility. Every broken heart taught me the value of love. Every meanness shown me only made me appreciate kindness all the more. Every betrayal taught me about true friendship. And every time I was slandered and had my life damaged by lies taught me dignity. No, there is nothing to forgive. Nothing."

That night I dined at 8 p.m. and enjoyed the most wonderful meal and company of my life. When I asked politely for a third serving everyone roared with laughter. And so did I. You see, I was home.

{ 5 }

The True History of Australia (Part 1)

S ome time ago an Italian sea captain got lost and
discovered a vast incontinence. Then some Dutch
people, probably Vikings or Ewoks, killed him and
hid the body under rocks in Sydney. That's why

it's now called the famous Rocks area and so many Italian restaurants are built there. Captain Francesco Albineani is somewhere underneath them. True story. I think.

The Vikings raped and pillaged, as they do, then went home and forgot all about The Demons Land, as they called it.

A short time later the English arrived and, owning a lovely flag, planted it in the ground and claimed ownership. Some of the Aboriginals were not happy about this technicality, but when they raised concerns, Captain Cock put them in their places by saying, "Well you can't bloody speak English that's why!"

Not long after creating this bad karma, Captain Cock himself was killed, along with his crew, on another expedition to steal countries, and was turned into a sandwich by a group of tribesmen who, after viewing his thin white legs, mistook him for a chicken. That place is now called the Sandwich Islands. It was thought that the Chicken Islands was a little disrespectful to what had been great semen.

Somewhere around this time an angel appeared to King George The Turd, known to be completely bonkers, and said, "You must rename this lovely country. It does not deserve to be called The Demons Land."

King George the Nutcase, quick as a late train, said, "Well what do you suggest, oh vision?"

To which the Angel replied, "Call it Orrrrstraalia."

King George said, "How do you spell that?"

The vision replied, "I don't have a fucking clue, I'm an angel, dickhead!"

And that is how this vast beautiful incontinence, known for its floods, came to be called Australia.

Back in England someone got the smart idea to get rid of all the Irish in London by sending them to this new land. When the Irish said, "Fuck you, we're not going!" They were arrested on trumped up charges, such as your name was Paddy. Or your mother had two eyes.

Disgruntled, the Irish arrived here and haven't stopped whining. Or beering. Sometimes they sing irritating songs about it.

The Aboriginals, a very spiritual race, were forced to watch Irishmen drink until they fell down and got up again, urinating on dingoes and each other. The Aboriginals mistakenly thought it must've been some kind of weird ritual from the old country, and vowed to give them a wide berth.

One of the Irish flock, Edward Kelly, known to his mates as Pansy, kicked up such a fuss about being in the Land of Incontinence the Victorian Police targeted him as a "arsehole" and offered him a job. They explained that if he wanted to be in the force he'd have to drop the name Pansy and be called something boring like Ned.

Well, Neddy told 'em what to do with their job and stole a horse, riding off into the horizon yelling, "Catch me if you can you drongo coppers!" He was followed for miles by the Police in their attempt to explain to the mad bastard that he'd stolen his own horse which was not quite an offence in anyone's book. Even if you were Irish. Pansy Ned, short time later, teamed up with a nice man sporting a sensible haircut named Joe Byrne, a former dress maker of some note. As Ned had a habit of trying on ladies' dresses and staying in them for some days, the two young men had much in common and hit it off immediately.

Finally, the Police said, "That's it, we've had enough of Pansy Ned stealing his own horses, and setting fire to his own house (with his Mum and sister in it), that we better put him away for his own safety." That's when Pansy Ned and Joelene (as he was now named) Byrne hatched the idea, after four bags of funny mushrooms on toast, to make a suit of armour. Possibly a great concept but like all things Irish, deeply flawed. The young men, tripping off their tits, forgot about covering Neddy's legs. Some say it was a miscalculation, others say it was Ned's vanity that was his undoing. Ned sent word to the coppers that he was intending to ambush them (on reflection possibly a fatal mistake tipping them off). He then forwarded them all free train tickets to Glenrowan. This, even the Victorian Police, world famous for their stupidity, thought was curious and got their accountants in at once to add two and two together. What followed was a big showdown at Glenrowan between Ned and a few of his mates, Mick Jagger and Heath Ledger, against the entire Victorian Police Force. Now, even though the coppers were dull, it only took a few hours for them to work out that if they aimed at Pansy's pins they could bring the arsehole down. Ned's last words were reportedly "(I would've made) Such a wife."

In the continuing chapters I will document with the same passion for accuracy and historical detail the lives of other such incredible Australians as General George Armstrong Custer, Billy The Kid, Ronald McDonald and Gandhi.

FH

{ 6 }

The Hit Man

He had ended up in Van Nuys. A crummy studio apartment with a bed in the living room along with everything else. Well, what there was left of his life. The books, DVDs, unsold screenplays (some had come very close to being produced but that's a long story and everyone in this town had one), deteriorating videos, clothes that were fashionable a decade before, and letters from his father. The other two rooms were a closet, and a bathroom. He used the closet as his workspace where he'd set up a little desk and his temperamental PC. It was the dream room and like his dreams the rooms that housed them were getting smaller.

He would sit there sometimes all night writing a new screenplay in the hope that he could write his way out of this downward spiral he found himself on.

He also worked various part time jobs in order to pay the rent and buy some cheap food. He tried to keep busy to take his mind off the cold hard reality of the situation. If he thought too much about it he suffered panic attacks. He was far from home. And alone.

In April of 1997 he had landed in Los Angeles, full of excitement and fuelled by a motivation that he was going to take this town and knock it on its ear.

He'd saved enough money to comfortably get him through a year. Maybe two if he was frugal. Back home in Australia he'd been quite successful. A hit play here, a well received film there; even a few critically acclaimed books.

On paper he seemed to be someone to watch. There are no damned seasons in L.A so its easy to have years slip by you. And slip by Jonathan Tarney they did. His father gave up on him ever coming home. Then the old man gave up on life. Jonathan couldn't even afford the airfare to return for the funeral and his mean-spirited sisters hadn't offered.

Jonathan had started out living in fashionable West Hollywood, then moved to a sleazy part of Westin Boulevard, then to Sherman Oaks, then to his present rat hole in Van Nuys.

He'd been married, briefly, to an actress, but she gave up on his dream, and then him. She'd realized she needed to hitch her wagon to someone more substantial before her assets expired. And then one day she just left.

Jonathan came home to an empty apartment with some promising news but there was no one to share it with. So he bought a bottle of Jack Daniels. He bought one the next day too. He bought so many he never got around to polishing his script for the interested producer and the deal went away. Just like his wife.

His spiral accelerated after that. He couldn't help thinking that there was a weird, exciting feeling about free falling. The bills piled up and so did the empty bottles and all he could do was sit and look at them through hollow glazed eyes. He now had much in common with his father. They were both dead. Just in different ways.

When he was especially maudlin he'd re-read some of his late father's letters pleading with him to come home. He wanted to cry but tears didn't come anymore. Tears belonged to the living. Those that could be hurt.

One day while he was walking down Sepulveda Boulevard to the 99 Cent Store to buy his canned foods for the week, he saw a notice on a strip joint door advertising for a bartender. He pushed on the door and stepped inside the dark cavern of a place and stood there until his eyes adjusted and he could make out a few shadowy figures. One of them, a rotund shadow, said in a gruff voice, "What do you want? We don't open for a few hours. Come back later."

"I'm here about the job," answered Jonathan.

"Oh? You're a bartender?" said the rotund shadow man who walked into a pool of light.

"Well I've had some experience. Years ago. Back home. I was pretty good at it then. Well, so people said."

"My name is Louis Moretti. I own this place." He looked Jonathan up and down and smiled.

"Yes, yes, you may well be the answer to my prayers."

"Pleased to meet you, Mr. Moretti. My name is Jonathan. Jonathan Tarney," giving a smile he'd usually reserved for producers.

"Hey guys, I like Jonathan already. Unlike you bums this guy has manners. Have a seat, Jonathan. Tell me about yourself. You mentioned home. Where's that?"

"Australia."

Louis Moretti's eyes widened. He was impressed. He wasn't sure he'd ever met an Australian before.

"Well how about that? Did you hear guys? Jonathan here is from Australia. You guys are fearless aren't you? You know Paul Hogan?"

"No. No I don't."

"You know how to make a dirty martini?" Moretti laughed, and so did his shadow men. "Yes I do."

"Well what say you make me and the boys some dirty martinis and we'll talk money."

By the time Jonathan exited the place two hours later, and after making enough exotic drinks to impress Moretti and his associates, he had a new job. The money was good and he was also promised a small share of what the girls made each night.

Jonathan breathed a sigh of relief, walked past the 99 Cent Store and went into Ralph's Supermarket instead. A celebration was called for, so he purchased some cans of food that actually had names on them, and some real vegetables as well as some meat. It'd been so long since Jonathan had tasted a steak that he was beside himself with the excitement of a child. Hang the expense, he even grabbed a bottle of red to accompany his meal. He felt rich and tears welled in his eyes at how little it took these days to fill him with such euphoria.

How far had he fallen? All the pride and ego had long been trampled out of him and suddenly he felt like the luckiest man in the world. Yes, he could still cry. He was still alive. And he was going back to his apartment with a car full of groceries. Just like real people do.

That night he sat on his bed and ate his perfectly cooked steak and assorted vegetables, sipped his budget-priced but nice red wine and thought of his ex-wife. He wondered where she was and if she was happy. As happy as he was at this moment. He hoped so. All the anger was gone now and all he remembered was that he had loved her deeply and, for a time, she had loved him. In the end that's all that mattered isn't it? He would've loved tonight to phone her and wish her well but he didn't have her number anymore. He was no longer considered a friend.

He turned on the TV to watch something mindless so he wouldn't have to think.

This town had a habit of shrinking your dreams and your expectations down to size. If you were weak you got broken. If you were a survivor, you learned to appreciate any crumb that fell from the table.

Jonathan Tarney became a very popular guy at the Tits! Tits! Tits! strip joint on Sepulveda Boulevard. The customers liked him, so did the working girls and, more importantly, so did Mr. Moretti and his associates. Jonathan was making good money and had even been able to afford a bigger apartment. This one had two bedrooms and Jonathan converted one into his office where he occasionally attempted to write his great screenplay. The one that would make him a household name. Well, an industry name at least. He wasn't sure the public really cared about who wrote the latest hit movie. He wasn't completely convinced that many even realized they were written. What did it matter? Perhaps he just did it out of habit. Or to prove to himself that he was good at it even if no one wanted to give him a break. He smiled at the fantasy that one day, after he was gone, they'd discover his work and regret their stupidity. Then the more sobering thought entered his mind that all his work would be thrown out into the trash along with the other possessions of a man nobody really knew or took seriously.

For some weeks Jonathan had noticed that Mr. Moretti had seemed troubled. Not his usual self. Jonathan was fearful that perhaps his boss had taken a dislike to him or maybe one of his associates had complained about something he'd done. Paranoia haunts the desperate and Jonathan was panicked that his job would be taken away from him and he'd be banished back to the free-falling spiral and the anxiety attacks about the next rent payment.

A few nights later, one of Mr. Moretti's shadow men, Joe Camerilli, came over to Jonathan and asked him to stay back and see Mr. Moretti when he'd finished closing out his bar takings for the night.

"Sure thing," beamed Jonathan, trying to sound and look upbeat, but Camerilli's expression didn't change. It gave nothing away.

At the end of the night, Jonathan nervously made his way to Mr. Moretti's office. He knocked. "Come in," barked Moretti. Jonathan stepped in and closed the door.

"You wanted to see me, Mr. Moretti?"

"Yes. Yes, Jonathan."

With that, Moretti got up and walked over to the door and opened it. He peered out, checking that everyone had gone. He then closed the door and returned to his chair behind his big mahogany desk. His face was grim.

"Have I done something wrong, Mr. Moretti?"

"No. No, not at all. I love ya, Jonathan. I feel you're the son I never had. I really mean that."

Jonathan was suddenly so relieved he felt light-headed and exhaled his tension.

"But you can help me. I'm relying on you. I have a problem that someone needs to fix and I am willing to pay for it."

Jonathan waited for him to elaborate but nothing came. Moretti just kept looking at his talented bartender as though trying to read his every thought.

"Of course, Mr. Moretti. You in a way saved my life – or what was left of it – and if I can help you you know I will."

Moretti smiled. It was his turn to feel relieved.

"I knew I could rely on you, Jonathan. You have an honest face. That's why I liked you the first time I saw you. Remember?"

Jonathan smiled at the memory. He was feeling relaxed now, and loved.

"I need a man killed." Jonathan thought Mr. Moretti was joking so he went ahead and laughed out loud. When Mr. Moretti didn't laugh, the cold reality set in that he was serious.

"Are you joking?" asked Jonathan, already knowing the answer. "I don't joke about a man's life."

With that, Mr. Moretti opened his drawer, brought out a revolver, and gently placed it on his desk.

"This is an unmarked gun. It cannot be traced. You have my word on that."

"But I can't kill a man! That's not who I am."

"You would be surprised what we are capable of, Jonathan, when the situation arises."

Mr. Moretti got up and started pacing the room as he spoke.

"There is a man. A very bad man. And he is threatening my life, my livelihood, and that of my family. I cannot accept that or wait for him to strike. I must strike first. You understand?"

Jonathan clearly didn't.

"If I was to tell you all the things this man has done you would hate him as much as I do. He has killed men, women and children. I kid you not. Answer me one thing, Jonathan. If you had've had the chance to shoot Hitler would you have done it and saved all those peoples lives?"

"Of course but ..."

"Of course you would. This man is not Hitler but this man is evil. He is capable of hurting me, those closest to me and a lot of innocent people. Good people. Maybe even you. He is nuts. There's no telling what he'll do or how many people will step into his line of fire."

"Mr. Moretti – I am not a killer. I make drinks, I write screenplays nobody wants. That's about it."

"That's why you're perfect. No one knows who you are. No one would ever suspect you. As far as the police are concerned you don't exist. I had someone do a check on you. You're clean. You're not on their radar for anything. I am willing to pay you a hundred thousand dollars. Hear me? You could turn your whole life around on that, Jonathan. You could go to Mexico, buy a big house and live like a king the rest of your life. No more worries, no more pressures, no more hassles. You'd be free and clear."

"And what if I fucked it up and got caught?"

"There's no way that's going to happen. This guy takes the same route home every night. He's like clockwork. He has a driver we've gotten to and we know that on Monday night he will reach the corner of Van

Nuys and Vanowen at 8.30 p.m. The driver will stop at the cross section. When he sees you approach he will slide down onto the front seat giving you clear access to our man. You will be wearing gloves and empty the contents of the gun into him. You will drop the gun down the water drain on that corner and walk away. Not run. Walk. A block east will be a car with no number plates waiting for you. You will be driven to a hotel on Ventura Boulevard where there'll be a suite waiting for you. No need to report to the front desk as you are already checked in under a false name. Then next morning you walk out of the room, have breakfast at Jerry's Deli and catch a cab back to your apartment."

"I can't take someone's life. Even if they are evil."

"I think you can, Jonathan. Think long and hard about how good I have been to you, and what you can do with all that money. Don't think of yourself as a killer. Think of yourself as a soldier. And this is a battle. And you have the chance to save your father. I'd like to think I've been like a father to you. Haven't I? Well?"

Jonathan's head was spinning. Mr. Moretti wisely sent him home to think about it.

Jonathan couldn't sleep. He couldn't sit, he couldn't stop pacing, he couldn't comprehend what had happened and what he'd been asked to do. At 5 a.m. he drove to an all night liquor store and bought a bottle of Jack Daniels. By 8 a.m. it was gone.

Now he was drunk and it was time for the devil to whisper into his ear, "Think about what you could do with a hundred thousand dollars. Go to Mexico, buy a beautiful house, maybe get married again and have someone love you. You deserve it. You have had a hard life. All you have to do to change things is say yes."

At 9 a.m., still drunk, Jonathan phoned Mr. Moretti and said yes. The wheels were turning now and couldn't be stopped. Jonathan hung up and had the feeling of free falling again. Only his Maker above knew how this would turn out. His hands trembled as he realized he was placing the biggest bet he'd ever gambled with; his own life. He wasn't sure if the death penalty still existed in California for murder. He wasn't even sure if he preferred death to a life behind bars. He frantically tried to get those thoughts out of his head.

This had to work. It just had to. He was going to kill a man who didn't deserve to live. He was doing society a favour. That's right. Step from the shadows, identify the subject and say goodnight. That's all he had to do to be free and clear the rest of his life.

Mr. Moretti treated him like a son the rest of the week. Even the shadow associates were friendly to him, smiling and nodding their head with a new found respect. Jonathan liked being treated this way. It had been so long since anyone took him seriously.

He tried to get more information on the man he was to ... meet on the corners of Van Nuys and Vanowen but Mr. Moretti and his associates thought that was a bad idea. It was best to know as little as possible about the subject, they assured him. All a hit man ever wants to know is the routine of the person involved and what they look like. The less you know, the less emotionally involved you are. It is just a job. All Jonathan needed to know was this man was evil and had done despicable things.

On the intended night, Jonathan waited in the darkness. He checked his watch. It was 8:25 p.m. He realized that there was a man approaching who had but five minutes to live. Tonight Jonathan got to be God – it was in his power whether someone lived or died. He wondered how long ago it was ordained that his path would lead him to this spot on this night.

He nervously fiddled with his leather gloves and pulled the gun from his inside coat pocket. He attached the silencer he'd been given and gazed down the street. His heart was beating so fast it was like he was overdosing on amphetamines. Then the headlights of a big black car became visible in the far distance. The driver was good, he was right on time. Everyone was playing their parts in the play to perfection. It felt like it was meant to be.

There was no going back now. He knew too much. If he didn't go through with it he'd probably pay with his own life. His only option now was to put the bullets into the man in the backseat of the approaching car, or put one in his own brain.

The big black car came to a halt at the corner. Jonathan moved from the darkness and strode towards the vehicle. The driver on cue slid down and sprawled across the front seat. Jonathan was now close enough to see the face of the man in the backseat. He was about sixty-four with silver hair slicked back. He looked confused at the actions of his driver and said something inaudible. He then looked over and saw Jonathan approaching him. It only took him a split second to realize that something bad was about to happen and his last look was of great sadness as he grimaced and awaited his fate. Jonathan emptied his gun into the man, disposed of his weapon and walked away as instructed. It had all gone so smoothly it added to the whole feeling of everything being unreal. As Jonathan walked to the waiting getaway car it sank in that he was a murderer.

He couldn't identify the feelings racing through him. Was it shame? Guilt? Or empowerment? All he knew was there was so much adrenalin pumping through his veins nobody had better get in his way. Not tonight.

He got in the car and his driver sped off. Ten minutes later Jonathan was alone in a hotel suite watching a re-run of "I Love Lucy" and registering nothing. The snappy dialogue couldn't drag him back from his own conscience.

The next morning it was on all the news programs. They flashed photographs of Albert Esposito across the screen and showed footage of him with his family at his daughter's wedding. He looked so proud and happy. He gave a speech about the meaning of love that broke Jonathan's heart and he bowed his head and sobbed. He continued to sob through all the tributes from the community and local politicians who praised their fellow committee member for his efforts to clean up the district and shut down the sleazy strip joints and pornography industry that thrived through corruption of authorities and the sales of illegal drugs.

It was reported that his last words, according to his driver, were for his children, "Tell them I love them." This was the evil man? The man who'd been compared to a local Hitler?

Jonathan spent an hour in the shower trying to wash away his guilt. If he'd still had the gun he'd have used it again.

If Jonathan had've written the screenplay, he may've had an ending like this ...

It was the perfect crime. He had gotten away with it. He was free and clear and living in a little sleepy village called Amidic that rests on Lake Chapala in Mexico. He has a large mansion with a guesthouse and a swimming pool. His wife is much younger than him and is a beauty that also possesses a beautiful soul. She genuinely loves him and they are expecting their first child. There is a large photograph of Jonathan's father in the living room and he seems to be smiling with pride at everything his son has achieved. Life couldn't be more perfect. At last Jonathan is home. Slow fade to black and the credits roll.

Back in the real world, a man walked into the Van Nuys Police Station at 11.27 a.m. and confessed to the murder of Albert Esposito. He told them the whole story and later that day Mr. Louis Moretti was arrested.

The news was broken at 6 p.m. The anchorperson described Mr. Jonathan Tarney as a failed screenwriter.

{ 7 }

Two Thousand Dollars

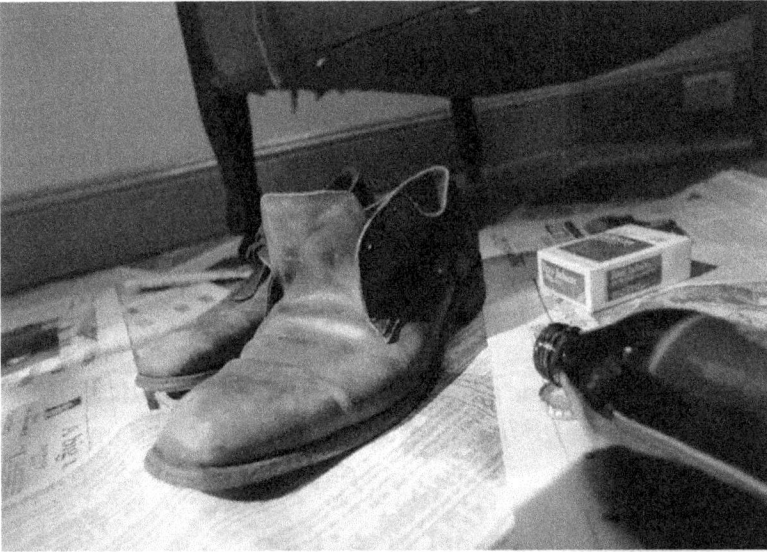

"**I**'m sorry Reggie but, after this, you're on your own."

Reginald Lesley sat in the head office of Newman & Son Publishing and listened to Michael Newman admonish him. A boy humiliating an old man. A man who had once been someone. Reginald looked around the office at the old dark wood

furnishings and floor-to-ceiling bookshelf that contained
most of the successful books this old and respected
company had published over the years. It contained five
of Reginald's books. He couldn't help think that there
was no way Michael Newman's late father Harold
would've spoken to him in this manner. Harold had
adored Reginald and was honored to publish the great
author's books. But that was years ago now and young
people had no respect for the past.

Reginald could've argued that his early success
helped this company survive in the competitive book
market. But why waste your breath or humiliate yourself
any further by having to justify your worth?

"Reggie?" Reginald hated the young man
addressing him in such a familiar manner. What did he
know about him? Really know? Or really care?

"Reggie? Are you listening to me? After this two
thousand dollars that's it. No more advances. We've
been waiting for you to deliver a new book for ten years.
You must admit we've been patient with you."

"It is almost finished, I assure you," croaked
Reginald. "You've been assuring us that for years. Every
time you want another advance. But no more. It's done.
Take your money, go and don't enter this office again
unless you have a manuscript in your hand. Am I clear
about that?"

If Reginald had still had any pride left he'd have
risen and hit the young man, but it was long gone. He
was weary and old and poor. He often wondered where
all his money had gone but after three wives and three
houses given away it was easy to see how it all
dissipated away like a mist.

Reginald held his temper and picked up the
cheque with a shaking hand. Once it was safely in his
pocket he looked at the young Michael Newman with

contempt and sauntered to the door. Just as he was about to exit he heard Michael's final jab to the heart.

"Oh and Reggie, you can't die for at least another 10 years. You owe us too much money. We need at least another three books out of you to clean the slate of debt."

Reginald opened the door and left. He walked along the corridors towards the elevator and thought about the old days when he came here and how everyone was in a state of excitement at his arrival. Young secretaries blushed and flirted with him, executives rushed to shake his hand, and Harold Newman addressed him with the hushed tones of respect.
Gone. All gone. And how he wished he was gone too. Now Harold's young upstart of a son had sentenced him to another 10 years of this life.

Reginald had no idea how he could survive once this two thousand dollars was gone. There was no new book, let alone another three. He was all written out. He'd sold short in the boom and now lived in downtown purgatory.

He walked out onto the city street and just wanted to get lost in the sea of moving bodies. No one noticed him anymore and that was a great relief. He'd hate those that'd known him to see what he'd been reduced to. Little more than a beggar in a worn out suit. His shoes were worn too and had holes in them but he covered those with newspaper. The only thing the dailies were useful for these days he thought.

He went to a cheap diner restaurant and ordered the $10 lunch which came with a soup.

The young waitress was always nice to him and he so appreciated her pretending to care about this old weary man. Her name was Noeline and he wished he had some money to leave her in his will. But there was no money. And soon there'd be no him. He had it all worked out now. Once the two thousand was gone he would follow and go too. He had to. There were no other options for him. He was acutely aware that he'd passed his use-by date and every day that belief was confirmed by the life around him. Life had been a series of small deaths and in a way he was well prepared for the final one. What took up most of his day was trying to work out the best way to make his exit. He didn't want it to be messy. It should be dignified, like he had once been. He smiled thinking that the reports of his death would probably trigger some healthy sales on his past catalogue of novels and that even Michael Newman may be pleased at the results. Might even pay back all the advances.

Noeline came by his table and conspiratorially slipped him an extra bread roll. She was a lovely girl, he thought, and wished he'd have met her in his prime. Life is so unfair and taunts us with such things.

He finished his coffee and stolen bread roll and headed home to his shitty room to watch some shitty TV. This meal would have to last him three days until his cheque cleared at the bank.

He figured that this two thousand dollars, if he was frugal, would be gone by August. He wasn't sad. He was actually looking forward to a nice long rest and catching up with some old friends on the other side. He couldn't wait to tell Harold Newman what an asshole his son was.

He had left a manuscript addressed to Michael Newman that consisted of "Fuck You" typed 20,000 times and regretted that he wouldn't be around to see the expression on his rat-like features when he started to read it.

By the time Reginald got home to his rented one room in a large cold house occupied by young people, he was exhausted and took his tie off and unbuttoned his shirt. He also slipped out of his shoes, laid on the bed and switched on his old portable television set. He changed channels until he found a nice black and white movie to watch. It was set in an era that he understood and the story was about a writer. He was young, witty and clever and all the women wanted to be with him. He was so wealthy and successful and everyone paid him great respect. The scenario seemed like a comforting fantasy to Reginald. Sometimes he wished he lived in a Hollywood movie where people never got dirty, or had their money taken, and there was always a happy ending. The guy always got the girl. The right girl. And they lived happily ever after and their love never died.

Twenty-five minutes into the movie, Reginald Legley passed away; the two thousand dollar cheque still in his coat pocket. At last God and he had agreed on something – it was Reginald's time to go. They'd just differed on it by a few weeks. His body would not be discovered for three days. And only then because someone who rented another room finally complained about his TV set being on all night.

Michael Newman was stunned by the press and public reaction to this old man's passing. Reginald was hailed as one of our greatest writers and there were several features detailing his life. All the good stuff. The young man who ran Newman & Son Publishing was taken aback by the respect paid to this man. An old man he'd recently degraded and stripped of his last layer of dignity. One layer too much.

Noeline wondered what had happened to her favourite customer, the old man who liked to sit in Booth 14. She hadn't known who he was but sensed that he must've once been someone special. She just felt it and wished she'd known him better. He acted like he knew things.

{ 8 }

The Dream Date

Tim O'Reilly's hands trembled as he dialed the number. Her number. Christine Milchem had been the prettiest girl at his high school. A goddess. He had fallen in love with her at first sight and that love had lasted twenty years this January. They had dated a few times during high school and he remembered floating in her presence as if it was a dream. Sometimes, over the years, he had wondered whether it actually had been a dream. Thankfully he had a photograph of them at the Lobster Cave to prove it wasn't. They had looked good together. Well, so he thought. A handsome couple with life before them. But Christine got a job overseas and Tim stayed at home to pursue some ambitions that wasted him some of his best years. Life was funny, wasn't it?

He had heard that Christine had married some guy and they'd lived in New York for some years before he got caught with his secretary. Tim married a girl named Lynette who understood him for two years of their ten-year marriage. Then she hadn't understood him at all. They became strangers living under the same roof, going their own ways, not caring enough to even ask. Eight of those years had kinda been like a death. A nothingness. Tim often thought it was lonelier to be with the wrong person than to be on your own.

Well, now at last, he was on his own. There were no more distractions or detours, or certificates binding him to someone, he was free. God Almighty, free at last! A friend had informed him that she was back in town and Tim had tracked down her number. Now he was making the call. Perhaps the most important phone call of his life. Something he should've done years ago and stopped her from leaving him. If only he'd done so, he could've saved them both so much heartache. He was hoping that the time was now right and she would feel the same as him. Perhaps she'd pined for him too and had regrets instead of dreams every night.

It was ringing. His heart skipped a beat and he prayed he wouldn't have a coronary malfunction before he heard that voice again.

"Hello?" answered the voice, and he was suddenly a young boy again. But a young boy with wisdom. This time he wouldn't let her go.

"Hello, Christine? It's me?"

"Who?"

"It's Tim."

"Tim who?"

He faltered and so did his voice. All the bravado he'd mustered up for the call was draining away. "Tim O'Reilly."

"I don't know any Tim O'Reilly," she snapped, her tone suddenly that of someone talking to a telemarketer. He'd never heard that tone in her voice before.

"We went to High School, remember? Even went on a few dates. Remember our night at the Lobster Cave?"

"Oh Tim, you were the guy with the red hair weren't you?"

"No, that was Billy. I'm Tim. Remember the Lobster Cave? We both got a photograph of us there. What a night we had, huh? I told you to go ahead and order anything you wanted, hang the expense, we were going to have a night and create a lasting memory."

"I don't think I've ever been to the Lobster Cave?"

Now Tim was getting a tone, "Yes, Christine. You went to the Lobster Cave with me. I have the photograph. We had a wonderful time. You told me so. We held hands walking back to your place and we kissed. Admittedly not on the lips, you turned your head, but it was a moment. A magic moment. I held you in my arms and it all just felt ... right."

"Are you sure this is not Billy?"

"Fuck Billy!"

"I did actually. He was hung like a horse. Come on, Billy, stop kidding around. You were always such a joker. Y'know I've often thought about that night we had. Even when I was with my husband."

Tim wanted to vomit. This couldn't be Christine the girl of his dreams? She was sounding like a tart. Then relief set in. It was probably her sense of humor. He loved a girl with a sense of humor.

"Christine, it's me, Tim. Tim O'Reilly. Remember? I have brown hair. I was quite tall for my age. Used to play basketball. Stop with the kidding."

"Oh? Tim." The name Tim was uttered with a tone of disappointment not heard since the Titanic captain's response upon being informed he wasn't leaving the ship.

"Yes ... Tim. Remember me? I've remembered you. There hasn't been a day since that I haven't thought of you. Not a day."

"Whatever happened to Billy?"

"He's dead!" He was as dead as Tim's tone was.

"What? How?"

"A car accident. Killed three innocent people with him. He was always reckless. Do you remember that?"

Tim thought he heard her sniffling at the end of the phone.

"Thank you for informing me. That was very sweet of you. He was the love of my life. He really was. What was your name again?"

Tim was not sure he answered her. He was gone. Gone in so many ways that nothing much mattered or made sense anymore. He was sitting at the Lobster Cave. He thought it would be romantic to call her from there. He had ordered oysters, lobster and champagne. Exactly what they had chosen on their date.

He looked up bewildered and despairing. A waiter saw this and came to the table. "Would you like something, sir?"

It took Tim a while to answer. To even remember where he was.

"No. I want nothing else. I'm done."

Tim paid the bill and left. The waiter went to the table and realized nothing had been touched. Perhaps the poor man had taken ill. Oh well, the staff had a nice treat to look forward to at the end of their shift.

Tim walked out onto the pavement and watched the traffic zip by. The noise and the cold air felt good. He thought back to the last time he'd been here and how that young boy had worked a part-time job for weeks to be able to bring his dream date to this place. He now looked at it long and hard knowing he'd never be back. It was like his dream. Once it's been dreamed you can't go back. You must dream new dreams. There would be someone else. Eventually. If he was lucky. And this time he wouldn't let her go.

He walked home. All he knew was he hated Billy.

{ 9 }

Death Takes A Ride

I t was a black night and the only thing visible was the winding road lit by the high beamed headlights. Jeffrey Marshall had been driving for 18 hours now and was still a day away from his destination. His car radio had long lost any connection to local radio stations and he was beginning to talk to himself. Well, he thought he was. Perhaps his one-sided conversation was only taking place in his head.

"I've never seen a night so dark."

It was impossible to make out anything except the road ahead. It was eerie. It was like the only things that existed in this world were him, and the throw of the light. Before the radio died the last news bulletin warned about the possibility of a serial killer. It was the only thing that could explain the disappearance of 12 people in and around this area over the past few years. Jeffrey didn't want to think about that. He hated to dwell on things that were unexplainable. All he knew was that people were capable of very bad things. Even good people. And that there were no answers to anything. Well none that made sense anyway. Things were what they were and it was best not to send yourself nuts looking too deep into stuff. He checked his petrol meter and still had half a tank. This was not a place to run out of fuel. He picked up the speed as though wanting to leave this night behind him.

He turned a bend and suddenly there was light and smoke. And a shadowy figure waving him down. Jeffrey was tempted to keep going but it looked like the man had misjudged the bend and his car had landed in a ditch on the side of the road. Jeffrey, against his better judgment, pulled to a stop some distance from the crash. In his rear view mirror he saw the dark figure slowly walking towards him. The man moved in a way that was unnerving. He almost glided in slow motion. Jeffrey hated himself for stopping but he had no control. It was as though he was giving in to the inevitable, and there was a liberating feeling to that sense of free falling. Finally, the stranger reached Jeffrey's car and tapped on the side window. Jeffrey hit the button and the window came down. He looked into the stranger's face but the night, and the hood the man was wearing, hid most of his features.

"Can I get a ride with you to the next town?" asked the stranger.

"Of course," replied Jeffrey.

The stranger opened the door and got in. Jeffrey started up his car and they continued weaving through the black night.

"You misjudged the turn back there huh?" said Jeffrey, stating the obvious in an attempt to kick start a conversation. But the stranger said nothing. He looked straight ahead as though mesmerized by the light and the road.

"Are you okay?" enquired Jeffrey.

Again, there was silence. Just as Jeffrey was about to charge ahead with another question, the stranger answered, "Yes. I'm okay."

"Have you ever seen a night like this? It's pitch black. Not a star, not a moon glow, nothing," observed Jeffrey out loud.

"There is a light. Out there."

The stranger pointed to where the dense forest was to their left.

"A light?" asked Jeffrey.

"Maybe lots of them," answered the stranger.

"But that's impossible. There's nothing out there. I know this area well," answered Jeffrey.

With that, the stranger slowly turned his head to look at Jeffrey. Suddenly Jeffrey could see his features, his sunken dark eyes and a smile filled with the conceit of somebody talking to a stupid child.

"I know what I saw." answered the man.

"I'm just saying that there's no town or energy plant or anything that would be generating a light. That forest is very dense. It's a death maze. You got lost in there you'd never get out. So, where would a light be coming from?"

"Do you believe in aliens?" asked the stranger. Jeffrey looked at the man and suppressed his desire to answer, "Well, not until now." But he didn't. Instead he gave one of those answers you give when you can't be bothered considering such things. "I only believe what can be proven."

The stranger smiled again and said, "So how do you explain the light?" Now it was Jeffrey's turn to go silent and stare at the road ahead.

After some time, the stranger added, "And how do you explain 12 people gone missing from around here?"

"Oh that I can explain."

The stranger waited for the driver to elaborate but instead Jeffrey steered his car to the side of the road and turned off the engine. He shut down the lights and got out of the car walking slowly around to the passenger side and opened the door.

"What's this then?" asked the stranger.

"I don't really know. It's just something that happens and, like your lights in the wilderness, can't be explained. Now get out of the car please."

The stranger got out and rose to his full height. It was several seconds before he realized he'd been stabbed. Then again. And again. He felt the blood with his hand just to be sure. Then he looked into the face of Jeffrey Marshall. But there was no trace of conceit, or pleasure, or any discernible emotion on Jeffrey's face. The most unnerving thing was the sheer nothingness of what he felt and saw.

"Why?" asked the stranger.

"I stopped asking that a long time ago. It just is what it is."

Four hours later Jeffrey was back on the road. He was exhausted from the ditch digging and pushing the stranger's car off the road and someway into the forest. clothes were muddy. He'd have to stop at a motel, clean up, have some sleep, get dressed in some clean clothes and throw his bloody muddy ones into a nearby river. He felt some tingling of satisfaction watching them rush off towards the sea and wishing it was him. They were clean and free. Yet he was chained to this dirt. He had tried many times to stop but it was no use. He was good at it and it calmed him for a time. Then whatever it was inside him would build to it again. He had long ago accepted that this was his lot in life.

It was almost nightfall again by the time he got back on the road. It was another black night. He kept looking for answers in the final expressions of his victims but the truth is there was nothing. No anger, no fear, no confusion, nothing. Strangely, there was a peace. If anything, a relief that it was all over. Jeffrey justified his deeds as acts of compassion. If you believed in a God, then wasn't it destined that Jeffrey and his victims would meet on such a night? And that he would play his role as well as they played theirs. Wasn't Judas just as chosen as Jesus?

He suddenly thought about the lights in the heart of the forest that his most recent victim, Number 13, had seen. Had he been hallucinating? Was it a premonition and he was glimpsing the lights of heaven? "It doesn't matter. And it don't do any good to think about such things," said Jeffrey to himself.

Jeffrey had never seen a light in the darkness. Only a road. One that bends and goes on forever and, occasionally, along the way, things would happen.

FRANK HOWSON

{ 10 }

The Lonely Life

Harold Blimp had always been an actor. "I was born into this" he once said. The truth is he'd been treading the boards since his seventh birthday and that was some time ago, although he was loathe to reveal just how long. This business of show had given him so much. It had taken as much too, if not more, but it was useless to dwell on such things. To do so could numb you with pain and one must always be positive and ready for that next big break. This industry thrived on positive people – and if you couldn't be one you could always act it.

Tonight Harold sat in his dressing room and prepared for the performance. His whole life was about preparation. When he performed he had no time for anything else. Several wives had found that impossible to deal with so they were gone and here he was, still preparing. His day consisted of sleeping in until midday. He needed that sleep to recover from the previous night's performance and to fully rest his voice. He would rise and shower. Nothing refreshed him more than standing under a hot shower and he used to always say it was one of the great rewards in life. It seemed to wash everything away. Like a daily baptism. He dried and dressed and then strolled to the local coffee shop where he took breakfast every day. He was something of a legend there. The people who ran it remembered him from some of his television performances in the '60s and they treated him like he was still somebody. They were always bragging about him being a regular although not many found the name that familiar anymore. But out of manners to the kind family that owned Dino's Coffee Place most people acted as though they did.

He never read the papers as he did not want any distractions on his mind other than the mountain he was preparing to nightly climb – the performance. It was all that mattered. He would nod and smile at the lovely family that served him but they long ago knew the rules – he could not chat as he was preserving the voice. Eight shows a week and every one must contain the very best of him. One never knew who was out there in the darkness watching. Even at the matinees. In fact, he remembered the time Lord Olivier was present at a Wednesday matinee and came backstage to tell Harold how marvelous he'd been. Dear Larry had even asked

Harold if he'd come to London and join his National
Theatre troupe. Alas, Harold was married at the time
and, with one thing and another, he never got there. He
often wondered where his life would've gone if he'd
accepted Larry's invitation. Maybe he'd be receiving
Oscars and Tony awards and the like. But he believed in
God and that there was a reason for everything and that
God somehow wanted him to be performing at the
Elwood Players Theatre. Life was funny, wasn't it? The
way things work out. He consoled himself that going to
London may've made him a big star but he could've
wound up burned out and disenchanted like so many of
them. Here, at home, he was a big fish in Elwood and
unless he was delusional was convinced he was giving
some of his finest performances. In fact, only recently, a
young critic for the Elwood Times wrote that Mr. Blimp
"... gave what can only be described as a stunning
interpretation of King Lear revealing that Shakespeare
was right up there with Neil Simon when it came to
comedy and had us all rolling in the aisles."

Mr. Blimp was quite proud that the word
"stunning" had been attributed to his performance and
wondered why the producers had not displayed it in the
foyer. But they too were young and he was finding it
lonely that he didn't have too many people left his own
age to talk to anymore. Most of the people he talked
about or quoted were met with blank expressions by the
younger generation who seemed to only have a working
knowledge of the past five years. Tops.

After his two poached eggs on toast with a slice
of burnt streaky bacon washed down by a pot of coffee,
Mr. Blimp would bid his admirers at Dino's Coffee
Place a silent good day and wander the streets to clear
his mind and think through his impending performance.

Every minute of his day was dedicated to being ready to give his best at 8 p.m.

Sometimes memories would invade his mind and he would find it difficult to function. He would stop and passers-by would sometimes enquire if the old man was Alright. Especially when he started talking back to ghosts. He had apologized to Mildred so many times on street corners for not loving her enough. And sometimes he wondered how old his son was now and what he was doing. He had tried to get word to him on so many occasions but could never quite track him down. He hoped he didn't still harbor resentment towards his father. Didn't he know that every performance he gave was dedicated to him? And that all he wanted was his son to be proud of him and to one day admit that he was Harold Blimp's son. Maybe even use his real name and not his stepfather's.

Harold generally got to the theatre at 4 p.m., well before anyone else. He would walk the stage area and practice some of his moves and gestures. Then he'd sit in his dressing room and do his vocal exercises to warm up his voice. That would take an hour or so. Then the detailed make-up process would begin and he would transform himself from Harold Blimp into King Lear, or Don Quixote, or Shylock, or a father who was loved and forgiven.

At 7:45 p.m. Mr. Blimp would walk up the stairs to the stage level and stand in the wings. It was one of his rituals. He had so many rituals he needed a whole day to devote to them. Sometimes his second wife Gladys would pop into his mind and ask him why he'd betrayed her with her best friend. The stage manager was by now quite used to Mr. Blimp's nightly conversations with Gladys.

"I'm so sorry, Gladys, I don't know why I did that. I was just a silly young insecure man who didn't feel worthy unless I was loved by everyone. Silly young men make mistakes. I loved you, Gladys, I truly did. Isn't it time you forgave me? I have outlived everyone and there's no one left to forgive me."

"Are you alright, Mr. Blimp?" asked Jerry, the stage manager.

Mr. Blimp was jolted back to here and now and played the part of a man who was in total control.

"Why yes, Jerry, I'm fine. Just going over some lines. That's all. Us thespians are a mad lot, huh?"

Jerry thought that was an understatement but decided it was best not to reply lest he have an honesty attack.

"House lights down," Jerry whispered into his intercom. "Curtain! Mr. Blimp, your entrance." "Thank you, Jerry. You're a good boy."

Harold walked in the darkness to the centre of the stage and found his mark. As he stood in the dark awaiting his pool of light, Harold Blimp summoned up the energy from his soul to once more play a man who descends into hell – one who traded everything he loved for flattery – who was once a king but is now mad with grief.

FH

{ 11 }

The Critic

Arnold Beckman had been a critic most of his life. He had the knack for looking at anything and reducing it to a dismissive smirk. He had started his career at the Age as a sports reporter and his acutely analytical and cynical stories had gained much attention, and not a few enemies. But, most importantly for a career, he was talked about.

After the retirement of respected arts critic Colin Bednall, the editor thought it might be fun to throw the acid worded Mr. Beckman into the theatre and film world and see what results that would bring. Arnold Beckman hated his new job. Almost as much as he hated life. There were the endless movies that he tried to show up on time for, but if he was late he'd ask a colleague what he'd missed and from that whispered brief would write his dismissive review. Then there were the theatre shows, mostly revivals of things that had worked in the past. This hindered his style as it was difficult to find much fault with George Bernard Shaw, Eugene O'Neill, or that Shakespeare chap, so Arnold would have to dig deeper finding flaws with the new productions. Or casting. The nervous producers would wine and dine him before the shows and attempt to make small talk. Arnold found much power in silence and used it as he greatest tool. The less he talked the more nervous they became, and the more chance they'd say something foolish that'd give him the opportunity to pounce and belittle.

He toyed with people's lives. In some cases, he destroyed some promising ones. He enjoyed the young actresses who attempted to converse with him at after show parties. Some of the more naïve ones thought they could sway his opinion if they flirted with him. Those that knew no better would nervously find themselves back at his gloomy, untidy apartment, where they'd be stripped and made to stand naked in the middle of his room while he walked around inspecting them and giving his opinion. Some of these young girls would bear the scars of his poisonous words all their lives. It would be a long night for them. Arnold didn't much like the sex act. Instead the sacrificial lambs would be subjected to a series of humiliations while he gloated at how far they'd go to try and please him. In the morning they'd be

thrown naked into the corridor and then their clothes
tossed out after them. One final humiliation before
breakfast. Some of these young aspiring talents thought
so little of themselves, they'd return.

He hated driving so he travelled on the train,
avoiding peak hours so he wouldn't have to contend with
the public. He found them to be boring and nosey. He
had a woman come and clean his apartment once a week.
He paid her well as long as she did her work naked and
told him how much her husband disappointed her. That's
all. Sometimes her erotic talk would get her so excited
she'd beg him to touch her, but he would not. Most times
he'd read the newspaper while she pleaded.

Arnold had hated his parents. He'd been ashamed
of them and loved telling everyone he'd been adopted.
He never even took the time off work to attend their
funeral. After all, he had another disappointing film to sit
through and write a review about. He dined in
restaurants but food brought him no enjoyment. To him
it was not a sensual experience as some found it, but
rather the most mundane and common of efforts. The
need to replenish your body with fuel so it would keep
going.

He didn't watch television because the ads
annoyed him, followed by the programs that
disappointed him. Then there were the talk show hosts or
newsreaders that infuriated by looking down the barrel
of the camera and talking at him. He found it quite
unnerving. He found all eye contact to be so. He wore
glasses, not because his eyesight was bad, but as a
barrier, a guard, against other eyes looking too deeply
into him. He loved being hated. It kept people at a
distance. He was also thrilled at how intimidating others
thought him to be, and on opening nights he delighted in

entering a busy theatre foyer knowing that tension walked in as his companion.

He would've quite looked forward to death had it not been for the nagging suspicion that he, more than likely, would find heaven disappointing.

{ 12 }

Sherlock's Final Hours

I t seemed like the perfect time. The sun had almost slipped from sight, and the light was that thin thread between day and night. Holmes sat at his window and watched the approaching darkness with a morbid fascination. These days he had the time to do such things. The great detective was no more, because the great cases were no more. The only offers that came through his door nowadays only insulted his intelligence and belittled his talent.

He missed his genius nemesis Moriarty. There was no one to measure himself against anymore. By finally defeating him, the great Sherlock Holmes had signed his own death certificate. Like the greatest of duelists, they lived to outpoint each other, tingling with the excitement that the first one to flinch would be dead. They had given each other life, felt at its highest ecstasy. Everything after was a series of small deaths. Now Holmes was battling that most insidious villain of all – old age. When it attacks it attacks on all fronts, he'd remarked on occasion.

Life had now revealed how lonely it could be. He'd never gotten around to making friends. People only interested him if they were a suspect of some kind. The only companionship he had known was that of his associate, Doctor John Watson, a conservative man in all ways, who disapproved of the cocaine use, the untidy apartment, the late night violin playing and Holmes' short temper with potential clients. Although he wouldn't class him as a friend, Holmes had grown fond of Watson, and his plodding behavior sometimes amused him. In recent years, even Watson was gone. Lost to marital bliss – whatever that term meant. Holmes had scoffed when Watson had told him of his intention to take a wife, "Whatever for? Don't I give you enough problems to occupy your mind during our working hours?" But take a wife Watson did.

Even Mrs. Hudson was gone. Sometimes Holmes would try and remember her face but couldn't. He wasn't sure he'd ever really looked at it. Not really. She was just someone who was there. And now wasn't.

He had tried not to notice women. Even the most beautiful were denied a second glance. He feared them.

They were distractors from one's real purpose in life. To look into that abyss too long would render you the great nothingness of normalcy. The hypnotic funeral drumbeat of one's true ambitions. He often said of them, "How can any man build a foundation on such shifting sands?" He would never find out.

There'd only been one woman. The woman. He had solved every case but one. She'd outsmarted him. He'd underestimated her and her parting gift to him had been public humiliation. In a way he found it strangely exciting that she'd gotten the better of him. Not a day had gone by since that he hadn't thought of her and wondered what she was doing. Although he'd only seen and spoken to her several times, their relationship, in his mind, had continued for years. Once again he thought of her as night descended.

He rose from his chair, picked up his violin and placed it back in its case. There'd be no more music either. He walked to his desk and opened the top drawer. There was his only friend – the syringe. It was the only thing that could ease his mind and take him to a dream state where time stood still. He loved rituals and took great care with this final one. He fixed himself with enough cocaine to blow up most hearts, then went and sat back down by the window, looking out at the street life below. It was night time now. He heard some of the street boys running past, yelling at each other. Some taxi cab taking wealthy people to the opera. A prostitute negotiating with a loud drunk customer. And a baby crying.

It had been a grand life in many ways, he thought. But he was going now before he became an embarrassment to himself and those who admired him. He wasn't sad. In fact, he was calm and relieved. His heart and mind were now racing. His life flashed by yet he seemed to be able to savor every image as though being reassured he had truly lived. Seeing it all put together like this made him smile. Yes, it was a life indeed. And now he would get to experience the last mystery and solve that one too.

He was already gone when Doctor Watson knocked on his door at 9:24 p.m.

The next day the street boys would be selling newspapers detailing the death of the great detective. Watson was angry that the story had only made page three, but Scotland Yard had taken credit for most of the cases and Holmes was reduced to the status of a sometime adviser and "famous" eccentric. It was typical, thought Watson. He crushed the paper in his hands and ripped it in half. Nothing could subdue his rage. Then somewhere far-off he thought he heard his dear friend laugh.

{ 13 }

The Loss of Things

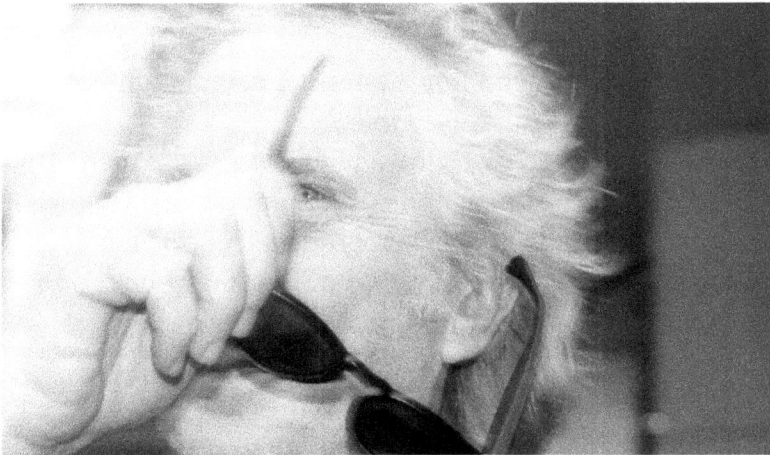

The man came home to find that a water leak had soaked many of his things. He got that jolting feeling one gets when you think you've walked into a nightmare but instantly realize it's all for real.

He then saw that most of his vinyl albums were seriously damaged and the covers, many of them signed by the artists themselves, were as much history as the memories.

Inside him the young boy that had excitedly bought these recordings, cried. But the old man standing here now looking at the damage stifled the urge to flinch. Instead he swallowed the pain like he'd swallowed most everything else in his life that he'd lost. Maybe the swallowing of pain explained his cracked voice. Perhaps it was the audible sound of a broken spirit.

Others were good at hiding the breakage. He wasn't. He'd been stripped bare.

He knelt and went through the records one by one, assessing the loss. Each cover brought back old times and he tried to feel as dispassionate as he could; like that of a surgeon; or a lawyer. That's right, take all emotion out of things until there is nothing to feel, that's the secret, otherwise God will punish you for caring too passionately about such things. Isn't it a commandment not to replace Him with false Gods?

Many of these recordings had inspired the man to become a part of the music industry. Some other damaged ones he'd later on even produced or written songs for. He'd always been proud of his name being on them. He used to, when he was young and naïve, excitedly point it out to people – until he realized some resented such success and the rest didn't really care. Now he tried to join the latter throng in not caring.

He couldn't help suspecting God had done this to him, and had many times in the past, to teach him the lesson that such things are not important. You come into this life with nothing and you leave with the same. The rest of the journey is preparing you for that reality.

What did it matter what was achieved? Pride was one of the seven deadly sins was it not?

Still, it would've been nice to have left some of these things to his son to prove that his father had done something. Anything. Proof of an existence.

He had lost people too, along the way. First his own dad, then his mother, then, for other reasons, his sisters. Then life took his son away to teach him the lesson that it is Alright to love something, but you are damned if you love that thing too much.

He joked that he had no family anymore other than the family of man. But it was no joke. It was his way of saying something important without crying. Maybe that's why his voice broke. It wasn't his voice that the break was in, it ran much deeper than that.

Ah, there was the album the great Del Shannon had signed for him. Oh, how he loved Del. Some months after he'd signed it, Del killed himself just as he was about to make a huge comeback. Why? Was the pressure too great and Del felt things too deeply too? He didn't know. He continued flicking his way through the records and the damaged memories.

A lot of people had stolen things from him. So much so that he was now too scared to show love for anything in case it was taken away. He felt parts of him were closing down in some weird kind of self-preservation. First his voice, now his heart.

Recently someone who'd professed to being his friend had stolen a framed program that Paul McCartney has signed. Paul had even personalized it by signing it "To ..." for him. The ex- Beatle knew how much he'd meant to the recipient. Now it was gone. Why would anyone want something with someone else's name on it? Even if Sir Paul McCartney did sign it? Perhaps the theft was intended to hurt. An act of envy. Or spite. Or bitterness.

Again, what did it matter? Everything goes, sooner or later. Then you go.

Quite a few women had gone too. He'd liked to say that they'd gone for various reasons but truth was, once the money ran out – so did they. The lesson, he thought, was make sure you fall in love when you're both poor, at least then you'll know it's for real.

Oh, and if you find someone genuine out there, hang onto them with everything you have, they're sure hard to find.

Some eventually give up looking. Even the most romantic amongst us learn to be still, sit tight, and watch the parade pass by.

He'd loved the circus as a child. One school holidays he'd gone to the circus with his mother and was so captivated, he found a way of sneaking back every day and seeing it all over again. Sometimes two shows a day. If you were small and walked in with everyone else it was possible to get in without paying and for a desperate boy on a zero budget, it was bliss. He loved the animals, especially the elephants, the trapeze artists gave him chills (and nightmares), and he laughed, along with everyone else, at the clowns. Even though they had painted upside down smiles on their faces, they gave everyone such joy with their foolish antics. Maybe that's where he learnt to keep 'em laughing and you'd be loved.

He wondered how such a little amount of water could've done so much damage. The irony was not lost on him that water cleanses and washes away. And perhaps that is what happened. The past was slowly being taken away, drip by drip, from him and replaced with the here and now. So many things had been lost in the flood over the years it was too painful to contemplate.

It made you tough. Strong. Clean. And in a strange way, liberated.

Water also baptizes you and taketh away the sins of the world. Or so we're indoctrinated.

All he knew was, there were no more records anymore. Symbolically, his record was clean. So he was free now to begin again.

Suddenly he felt like hearing the Beach Boys. Yeah, wouldn't it nice?

{ 14 }

And the Award Goes To …

Alex Winehauser was to receive an award from an industry that had long ignored or slandered him with lies and half-truths. Recently it had become embarrassingly obvious that Alex's omission from the history books of film was inexplicable and it was deemed necessary to give the old man something so he could conveniently stumble away and disappear. A trinket his son could inherit in a few years and display on a mantelpiece in some shabby suburban home. Or pawn.

Alex hadn't directed or written a movie in over 20 years and shunned all industry gatherings. A hermit living in a small bedsitter somewhere on the outskirts of Limbo. Those in the industry who'd once resented his youthful outpouring of product finally seemed satisfied that they'd long silenced him into oblivion and he was now safe to be wheeled out as a long forgotten has been. They were even secure enough to engrave on his award "For Sheer Brilliance." What did it matter anymore? No one remembered him anyway.

There was no greater film arts accolade in Australia than the A.S.S (Australian Screen Survivors) Award and they were even screened nationally in the non-ratings period and between football seasons. Alex had initially felt inclined to refuse it but his son had urged him to re-think that decision. As the momentous occasion drew close, Alex went to a formal hire store and rented a tuxedo and all the accessories. He spent most of next month's rent on it but felt that, seeing it would be his final public appearance, he should look the part.

His son noticed that his Dad wrote several drafts of an acceptance speech but tore most of them up. He was also observed pacing the living room floor and muttering to himself in angry tones. Occasionally he kicked a piece of furniture. Just when he'd thought he was out of it, they were dragging him back in. He was certain it'd be an uneasy night for all involved but they'd now agreed to play their respective roles and as such it was set. A masquerade of mutual congeniality.

On the eventful night Alex caught a cab but had it stop at a pub several blocks from his intended destination. He needed to calm his nerves with a few stiff vodka shots. Six to be exact. Now he felt he was ready for the lynching mob.

The awards ceremony was already underway when Alex made his noisy entrance and stumbled in the dark trying to find his allocated seat. He noticed the usual splattering of Aussie names who were obviously unwanted in Hollywood this week, as well as the familiar industry "observers." He sniggered to himself that the term "industry observer" was a polite title for people who did nothing but attend free events. Still, they seemed to know a lot about French cinema in the '60s. Finding his seat, Alex fell over someone's feet and landed to observe a local comedian, who'd never been in a film, being unfunny about tragic world events, and suppressed his urge to yell out "Fuck off wanker!" Instead, he thought he'd save it for his speech. The six vodka shots were really kicking in now.

Alex looked around and saw an actress, who'd once offered to blow him for a role, giving an impression of a sincere person smiling and waving at him. In recent years she'd become respected after being honoured with an award for her services to the industry. Tonight, she was sitting with a film critic whose claim to fame was once being married to someone who'd made a documentary that nobody saw. He scanned the room desperately trying to find the face of someone he liked but most of them had been so surgically altered that even their mothers would find it difficult to recognize them. Two rows from the front he saw the back of the head of a man who had ripped him off for a million dollars and now lectured on film integrity. Alex momentarily forgot he wasn't at home watching this circus on television and laughed out loud. The struggling comedian looked down at Alex and smiled thinking one of his jokes had actually worked.

The guest of honour felt claustrophobic stuck in the middle with clowns and jokers and unconsciously started to hum the Stealers Wheels hit song until he was ssssshed by an annoyed woman in the row in front of him. Alex had observed that she hadn't once laughed at the comic and was more interested in reading her program, no doubt speed reading to see if her name was mentioned somewhere. He couldn't understand why she was so annoyed at his humming when she was clearly not interested in the proceedings anyway. Then he realized she was at an age in her life when she was annoyed at everything, or at least, anything she could exercise some control over.

Alex looked down at his hands and wondered who they belonged to. He hadn't observed them closely in such a long time and now they seemed to belong to an old person. When exactly had this happened? Was the process ever so slow that one doesn't notice or does it happen one night whilst we're sleeping? The decline of a career was like that too. Alex had, over the past few days, tried to pinpoint just when his career ended and couldn't actually come up with a precise answer. One thing was for sure, the powers-that-be had cut off his lifeline a few years before he actually felt the aftershock. He'd been dead but just didn't know it. How ironic that these same people were now giving him an award. He suddenly felt like punching someone, anyone, but instead stifled the urge. The internal struggle to suppress his anger caused him to emit a low guttural groan from somewhere deep within his own abyss. The annoyed woman in the next row again turned to ssssh Alex but when she saw the expression on his face thought better of it and returned her attention to the comic dying onstage.

Alex suddenly stood. He wanted to leave. It took exactly one second to realize he couldn't do this as his son was excitedly watching the telecast with some friends and would no doubt be disappointed in him again. As a father he sat back down.

The comic ended his act, and possibly his career, to thunderous applause of relief from the thankful audience of snobs and has-beens.

Then, the organizers rolled out the big guns by announcing the next presenter, Olivia Koomash, one of the bright stars of Australian cinema. Olivia had made her name in all the usual suspect Aussie teen soaps on prime time as well as a few Aussie movies that critic Margaret Prune adored and everyone else had avoided. Australia's bright star was now a resident of Los Angeles and reading lots of scripts as well as sleeping with every sleazy producer in town. Her rent was paid by an old man she'd found on sugerdaddy.com and she was being seen at all the right places with all the wrong people. It was rumoured she'd once said "hello" to Julia Roberts. It was only fitting, thought Alex, that this girl had been chosen to introduce him. She was perfect. She didn't know him from a bar of soap and was born after his last film had been made. She even succeeded in mispronouncing his surname. No doubt the organizers had thought long and hard about this choice and it was designed to demean him one last time. It reeked of "If we have to give him an award let's make it as frivolous as possible" – giving the impression that Alex Winehauser's films had been pop in a classical world. This assumption had been compounded by his omission from most academic books published on the history of the Australian Film Industry. His films were not even mentioned in what were deemed to be comprehensive listings of all local movies. Alex knew this was not just his paranoia – these listings were compiled by industry "experts" who knew better. If it had been designed to hurt Alex it'd worked. It had damaged him in ways far greater than mere sadness or anger – it had broken his faith in human nature and the belief that at the centre of things was a goodness.

As Olivia Koomash waffled on about things she had no understanding of and continued to mispronounce words including some of the titles from his lifetime of work, Alex wondered, for the first time in his life, how and where one could purchase a handgun. It was one of those thoughts that are captivating for a few seconds until reality kicks in reminding you that, as a father, murder or suicide are not an option and are only a solution for those with nothing more to lose. Or to live for.

Alex was jolted back to the unreal world by the bubbly announcement of his name by Australia's new golden girl. She mispronounced it again but by now Alex had joined the rest of the room in not caring. Once, in his youth, Alex Winehauser had stood for things. Now he rose to his feet to stand for nothing. He was so conflicted that the applause sounded like surface noise on his brain. As he walked to the stage he was hit with an overpoweringly deep urge to vomit. And a realization. They had finally tricked him into selling out and condoning their appalling behavior. Accepting this award made him no better than them. In fact, worse.

He wasn't sure if he thanked Miss Golden Girl or not. Everything had seemed to blur for a few seconds. Lost. When he regained consciousness of the Here and Now he was surprised to see he was actually holding the award in his hand. He looked out past the bright lights to the shadowy figures in the auditorium and saw that quite a few had even risen to give him a standing ovation.

Perhaps they confused him with someone else. An easy mistake. Tonight he was actually someone else. The young man that'd made those films would've not been here tonight. He had principles. Alex heard the applause finally die down and then that deafening silence of dead air time. A message scrolled down on the teleprompter, "Say something!"

And in that few seconds it took Alex to draw breath, a miracle occurred. That young man, filmmaker Alex Winehauser, returned. He eyed the room as surely as Wyatt Earp took in every detail of any saloon he entered. And he began to speak ...

"I had a speech prepared but ... I tore it up." A few people laughed. Nervously. So far he was getting a better reaction than the opening comic.

"Creative people don't need awards. They need encouragement. It's scary being out there all on your own. Sometimes all you need is someone to say, "Just do it. I believe in you." You people, on the other hand, never ever believed in me. And here we are tonight co-conspirators in a big lie. This is not an award you wanted to give, it's an award you felt you had to give. You see, history has treated me better than you ever did. And now you're embarrassed. Well, I'm embarrassed too. Some of you people hated my films sight unseen. That tells me you hated me and what I stood for but in order to disguise your personal resentment you targeted my work. The thing I loved. The thing I lived for. The thing that made me get up in the mornings. But you're safe now. Alex Winehauser died 20 years ago. All that exists of him now is a pathetic old man who is so in need of love, even insincere love, that he got talked into coming here tonight. I often wonder what that young boy would've achieved if he hadn't been driven away. We will never know."

The teleprompter scrolled the message from the producer, "Just say Thank You and get off." Alex couldn't help but laugh, which confused the audience even more.

"I have been told to say thanks. Well ... I see out there in the audience Mr. Alan Foley, a man who worked tirelessly to see that my films never achieved the distribution they deserved. It was not enough for him to help bury me, so he has continued to bad mouth the corpse for the past 20 years. I sincerely hope it has brought you some pleasure, Alan. Now that we're old men it's important to feel good about ourselves. You know why we don't make great movies anymore? Because none of these fucking mean spirited and envious people ever encouraged anyone. That's what we're paying for now, folks. We reap what we sow."

Another message screamed across the teleprompter, "YOU ARE TAKING TOO LONG! AND STOP SWEARING!"

"I've been told to get off. So I will. What a shame, I had so many others to thank. As for this A.S.S Award – you can stick up your ass! You're safe now. I'm going home. There's only one person whose opinion means anything to me, and that's my son. I know he's watching this and I just want to tell him how much I love him. As a father I have taught him many important lessons for life. And this is just another. Hold on to who you are, young man. Everything you do, do for the right reasons. Fuck the awards. Fuck the praise. Fuck the criticisms. Fuck the phony friends. Fuck the history books. Fuck the money. For they will surely fuck you! Take it from one who knows. If my language has offended any of the 15 people watching this telecast tonight, I am very sorry but you can go fuck yourselves too! Good night, and thank you for having me."

With that, Alex Winehauser put his trophy (which resembled a glass dildo) on the podium and left the stage to stunned silence. He walked down the stairs, up the main aisle and through one of the exit doors. He was seen hailing a taxi in the rain. Then he was gone.

FH

{ 15 }

The Old Man Remembers

I remember when dinosaurs roamed the earth. About a hundred years ago now. Great fucking clumsy arrogant things – they crashed through everything and left us small creatures to clean up the mess – Well, guess what? They're gone and we're still here – Makes you think, doesn't it? Ah what do I know? ...They say I'm the oldest man in the world – well, what does that get you? Huh? A telegram from Elizabeth Vagina the Third of the House of Dimwits or whatever her fucking title is. I've had a few titles in me life – The only one I've held onto is "Fucking Idiot" – I'm quite proud of that title and wherever I go, even into unknown places –

all I had to do is start talking politics and sure enough within a few minutes someone will acknowledge who I am – I used to have a razor sharp memory – but now things blur together – I sometimes can't decipher between what I've lived, read, or dreamed – Well, that's what the doctors say – but what the fuck do they know, huh? – Let's face it, if they knew how to live why would they be studying someone's bowel? – You couldn't pay me enough, y'know what I mean? – My mind wanders, forgive me – But at least I've felt something, y'know? I remember being a small boy – and I saw Les Darcy, the greatest boxer ever, step out of the darkness of a doorway. He was dressed in a beautiful suit, collar, tie, gold fob watch – I stood there transfixed – He was magnetic – He turned and looked down at me and smiled that smile – the smile that would finally kill him – and walked away – Not a word was spoken and I'll remember it till I die – I hope to God that really happened and I didn't just dream it – I'm pretty sure it did happen – Life has robbed me of just about everything now – I can't walk – can't eat -can't have sex – can't remember what sex was like – all I had left were me memories – and now He's taking those away from me – You'd think He'd kill me outright rather than this sneaky stealing of things in the night – How come Darcy, who had everything, died at twenty-one and I'm still here? – Does it makes sense to you? – It sure as hell doesn't to me – But what do I know? – I'm the Fucking Idiot – But Life goes on – and for some of us – on and on – and on – I have a couple of kids – a daughter – and a son – Haven't seen either of 'em in years – Still, I heard they're proud of me – I believe they tell everyone their father's the fucking idiot – Sometimes I dream of them – and in my dreams they're beautiful in every way – But then again, so am I – That's how I know it's only

a dream – I do remember riding in the Kelly Gang – Did
I tell you? – I lived to tell about it, didn't I? – Told Ned
that the ambush at Glenrowan was a big mistake – He
told me to fuck off, so I did – It's lonely having the last
laugh – no one laughing along with it – kinda spooky –
Joe Byrne was a nice guy – So was Ned but his habit of
trying on ladies dresses was a little unnerving to us
country boys – He loved dressing up – Finally, he made
himself that suit of armour – great concept but like all
things Irish, deeply flawed – He forgot to cover his legs
– Now I know the Victoria Police are renowned for their
stupidity but – give me a break – it only took 'em a few
hours to work out that they could aim at his legs and
bring the arsehole down. And down they did – You
know what I mean? – I was invited to the reading of
Ned's will – I didn't know whether to be touched or
insulted when he left me his dresses – Anyway, in
shame I took off to America – I joined the Seventh
Cavalry under the command of General George
Armstrong Custer – Well, what a friggin' lunatic he
was, you know what I mean? – Looked the spitting
image of Errol Flynn in a blonde wig – I distinctly
remember saying to him in no uncertain terms – "Listen
Dickhead, there's six thousand fuckin' Indians down
there!" Well, he just gave me that stupid vacuous smile
of his and said "Alright then, let's be about it!" and rode
off, spraying me in mud from the hooves of his equally
stupid horse, Bigballs – Well, what the fuck does that
mean? – "Alright then, let's be about it"? – I fairly
quickly determined it meant "Let's get a hurry on and
get killed in the most-grisly fashion." Fortunately, I had
one of Ned's dresses in me saddle bag and I rode off,
side-saddle, in the opposite direction – I got about forty
miles before I ran into the James Gang and they gang-
raped me – Not the worst experience I've had – Still, I

did try tellin' them I was a man – seeing they were obviously too fucking dumb to work it out for themselves – but alas, I fell on deaf ears – I remember one of the Younger brothers grinning a set of decaying teeth and saying "Let us be the judge of that!" – I did and they never got back to me – It was a few days before I could resume riding side-saddle – but there I was – heading across the desert – a changed man – desperately traumatized – and crying into my perfumed hanky – I finally made it to Dodge City where I promptly bought some manly clothes and got drunk to prove I was ... well ... a man. In my present condition I was finding it easy to walk like John Wayne – I sang a popular song of the day, "Oh Mother, I've Just Had a Big Whopper and It Hurt Like Hell" and burst into tears – Fortunately someone in the bar recognized my royal lineage and called out "You must be a fucking idiot", to which I replied, "Yes. Yes, I am. And I am honoured to be amongst you." After that, their attitude toward me changed dramatically. Buffalo Bill walked up to the bar and said "You're the kinda gal I've been lookin' for" – To cut a long story short – I ended up having quite a successful career under the name of Annie Oakley – Let's face it, I wasn't the first person in show business to become a star by working in drag. Two years later I left Dodge City with some colourful memories, a love letter from Wyatt Earp, a different view of life and riddled with VD – This altered my thinking somewhat and I took off as a crew member of a sea vessel. The captain was a nice enough man – he had one leg and took an instant liking to me, much to the envy of the other sailors – Well, a few weeks into the voyage I realized we were sailing with a fucking madman. All he wanted to do was chase this fucking monstrously huge whale – I instinctively knew it wasn't going to end well

– He called the object of his obsession, "Moby." One night, having put up with hours upon hours of listening to him ramble and rage about this fucking boring old prick of a whale, I lost my temper and called it "Moby Dickhead." The Captain, Ahab, stopped and smiled. And, like everyone in showbiz, he had to embellish my idea by pissing on the tree. He shortened my idea to "Moby Dick." In my honour, he said. Of course, true to form, he told no one else about it and my contribution has been lost to history. Not, may I add, the first time I have been written out of a good story – Anyway, we chased that fucking whale until we couldn't remember what our names were anymore – Then, as moi predicted, that fucking spiteful blob said, "Enough is enough" and turned on us – Smashing the ship to the shithouse and taking the demented Ahab to the bottom of the ocean – All the crew perished except me – I was picked up some days later by a Norwegian whaling vessel and explained my story to them – I said, through an interpreter, that "... we'd all been fucked by a huge Moby ... Dick." I presume something was lost in the translation because I soon found myself back in the ocean. This proved to be a very trying time in my life. Still, what can you do? Fortunately, an English speaking person by the name of Bligh picked me up in his lifeboat. I asked him why he was rowing across the ocean and he confided that he'd too recently experienced a traumatic situation of which he could not elaborate. And, although he liked to whip me twice a day, we got on quite well and it was nice to be back in civilized company. I told him he bore a striking resemblance to Charles Laughton. He had no idea who I was talking about and it earned me another thirty lashes. But, having lived the life I had, I was painfully aware that things could be worse, and contented myself to looking on the bright side of things.

Bligh told me he'd never known another man to say thank you after a good lashing. I was a chirpy chap in those days. So appreciative of any crumb. We finally made it back to London and I got a job working for a detective by the name of Holmes. He lived on Baker Street with his "friend," Doctor Johnny Watson. I soon found out that my new employer was a raving coke-head and would stay up all hours of the night ranting about fuck-all. Several times I stumbled upon their late-night shenanigans – the two of them dancing around – Holmes looking like he'd dipped his sizable nose in the flour jar – with eyes like red pissholes. Creepy bastards. Made me long for Captain Ahab. Still, it was all good experience. I was able to draw on all this in my later life as a successful writer of children's stories. I wrote under the name of Enid Blyton. My first book, Nuddy in Boyland, created great controversy so the publisher changed the name to Noddy in Toyland. Couldn't help feeling something was lost, but still – it sold well. I felt that the discerning reader was still able to read between the lines and get something out of it. Unfortunately, my favourite character, Big Dick, never quite recovered from my publisher's molestation.

{ 16 }

The Three Wise Men

Once there were three wise men. No one was quite sure how they'd come to be called this. Rumours had it some Madison Avenue Advertising Agency coined the phrase for its three wealthiest clients. In much the same way as The Rolling Stones had come up with their own sound-bite catch phrase "The World's Greatest Rock'n'Roll Band" or Michael Jackson's self proclamation of "King of Pop." Anyway, the truth is the three wise men didn't do much, so it took some genius spin-doctors to attribute anything to them. The three wise men in question – Tony, Trevor and Alfonse – pretty much kept to themselves.

Having had the same mother in common they took to calling themselves brother. They lived in the groin of luxury in a huge mansion in some desert town near quite a well known mirage site. They didn't talk much so they rarely said anything foolish, which added to the advertising myth that they were in fact incredibly wise. Once, I heard on good authority, Trev said to Alfonse, "I reckon it might rain tomorrow." He was two years out on his prediction but what the hell? Pretty uncanny.

They had a bowling alley built in their mansion and played ten pin bowling all day, every day – except they played with nine pins because that tenth pin was always too hard to knock over. They watched reruns of "My Mother the Car" and wondered how any TV show could ever top this. Sometimes they skinny dipped with their clothes on. Most nights they phoned their local Chinese Restaurant and ordered kebabs. It was indeed a fat life.

One night Tony, who was bored watching the prawn channel, suggested that they should do something really important with their lives – like the Kardashians. The others mumbled their agreement and Trev was reported as saying "Oh wow" or words to that effect. The next day Alfonse phoned the government and instructed them to declare a public holiday so everyone could be as bored as the three brothers. One night, whilst sleeping after making love to his hand, Tony had a vision. St. Anna Nicole Smith appeared at the end of his bed and said "Couldn't help noticing what you were beating before and am quite impressed. Too bad I'm dead. Anyway, I have a message from the Supreme Unreal

Being who Controls the Universe, do you know who I mean?"

"Yes," stammered Tony.

"Elvis?"

"Oh man you are so smart. What a shame we didn't have children. Anyway, you need to wake your brothers and travel tonight on a long journey. There will be a baby born in a ghetto somewhere in the Bronx and this boy will one day be king. King of things most won't be able to comprehend. But, like Chet Baker, he will eventually die for our sins. How's that for a guilt trip on the world huh?"

"Can we leave Tuesday? There's a really good episode of 'My Mother the Car' on tomorrow night and it's one I haven't seen."

"No. You must do what the Supreme Being says and leave immediately. Timing is everything" said the lovely St. Anna Nicole Smith.

Finally, Tony accepted the calling and St. Anna bid him farewell. Well, after twenty minutes of making out.

Trev and Alphonse weren't very happy about being woken in the night, even if it was a message from Elvis. But Tony used all his powers of incredible persuasion and told them to move their "fucking asses or else!"

They hurriedly threw some garments into their Louis Vuittons and left by the light of the moon. The limo drive to the airport was grueling and then they had to endure the first class flight to New York watching newly made Hollywood shit on the inflight movie program, while being subjected to the terrible plane cuisine of Lobster à l'Américaine, washed down by a bottle of Louis Roederer, 1990 Cristal Brut, which Trev thought tasted like mouth wash. Oh how they craved to be watching their favourite movie classics like "Showgirls" or "Battleship Earth" and eating a chow mein pizza. They often wondered how the other half lived and pined to be like them. That poor lifestyle seemed so stress free and romantic.

They touched down at JFK International Airport and waited for their bags to be thrown up. Alfonse thought it strange that a former U.S. President would call himself after an airport. But, there was no time for such deep ponderings, they had a task at hand.

"So what is the plan now, Tony?" asked Trev. Tony blushed and his mind went all blank.

Two hours later, Trev reworded the question, "So what the fuck happens now?"

"I ... ash ... don't know. She wasn't big on details and I was too busy checking out her knock out body. I could see everything!"

"That's it" said Trev. "Last time I listen to any bloody message from Elvis. As far as I'm concerned he only recorded two good songs anyway."

"Hold on, it's coming back to me!" said Tony. "She said we had to go to the ghetto in the Bronx and wait for a little baby to be born." Trev and Alfonse calmed down when they realized that wouldn't be too difficult to achieve.

"I take back what I said about Elvis," said Trev. "I liked about four of his songs if the truth be known."

Outside the airport the three wise men saw a limo driver holding a sign that said KING. They realized this was a sign from Elvis and followed the driver to their limo. Within minutes they were off on the next leg of their incredible journey.

"Oh I remember another clue," said Tony.

"Do tell, do tell," asked Alfonse, who had a mental problem that sometimes made him repeat himself. "When I was making out with St. Anna she told me that when in doubt, follow the stars."

"Wow. Wow" said Alfonse.

"What was that like?" asked Trev.

"What? Following the stars?" asked Tony.

"No. Making out with a ghost?"

"Well I didn't get to third base because she said she was saving herself."

"What for? She waitin' till Tom Cruise dies or something?"

"Unreal. Unreal" added Alphonse.

"Where exactly in the Bronx do you guys want me to drop you off?" asked the limo driver.

"Just follow the stars," answered Tony.

"You guys need to get off the coke," muttered the limo driver. In what seemed like no time, they were in the Bronx. The limo driver spotted an actor that was once in "Welcome Back, Kotter" and said, "Okay you hippies, here are the stars."

"Oh thank you, thank you," said Alphonse and the three wise men exited the limo and stepped onto the streets of the Bronx.

It looked exactly like it was in all their favourite movies. Edgy, dirty, graffiti decorated and some lovely poor people were sitting in doorways. How quaint they thought it all looked. They wondered if the people who lived here knew how lucky they were.

"But where is the baby? The chosen one?" asked Trev.

"Yes, yes," added Alphonse. Tony slowly looked around and silently prayed to Elvis and St. Anna to show him the way. Just then, they heard a cry in the night. A baby was distressed. They turned and smiled to each other. It was indeed a magical night and they had all been chosen to fulfill it. They followed the sounds of the infant's wailing to a broken down old deserted tenement building. Manners would've had them knock on the door but there was no door. They entered, stepping over rubbish, and sleeping bodies of people old before their time. There, in a corner, was a young girl holding her baby. The three wise men knelt and honoured her by bowing their heads.

"We are humbled by you, dear lady," said Tony.

"We have brought you presents from far away," added Trev.

"I have a mental problem and repeat myself and my brothers are so much better than me. I'm sorry. I'm sorry," confessed Alphonse.

His two brothers looked at him as if for the first time.

"What are you saying, Alphonse? We love you and have always loved you. We think you are the smartest one amongst us and that's the truth," said Tony.

"Yeah. Who else knew that JFK named himself after an airport?" added Trev. Alphonse began to sob.

"Tonight I am filled with so much love for my brothers, and for you dear lady and for your child who the world has waited for – the world has waited for."

"It has?" asked the young mother.

"Oh yes," replied Tony. "An angel came to me and told me. Your son is precious and will grow to make us all proud."

With that they stepped forward and presented their presents.

"I give you all the money you need to educate your child and have a lovely warm place for him to come home to," said Tony.

Then Trev stepped forward, "I give you the health care to ensure that you and your son are always well."

Then Alphonse stepped forward, "I give you my love and friendship for as long as I live so that you know whatever you need I will be there for you. I will be there for you."

The young mother smiled and tears welled in her eyes. She held her son up so that he could gaze at the three well dressed men who were kneeling in his presence.

"Why, outta all the people in the world, have I and my son been so blessed?" asked the mother.

Alphonse was about to reply that she'd have to ask Elvis that, but his brother answered first. "You have not been blessed, dear holy lady, it is us who have been blessed. You and your child have given us the most precious gifts of all. Now we have something to live for. We have meaning in our lives. And our hearts, which were only a short time ago, a desert, are now filled with love."

There were no reporters present, publicists, or photographers to record the event. Their presence would've only devalued the miracle.

{ 17 }

The Business Lunch

I had been invited to lunch. A producer wanted to chat to me about my script and his plans for it. He had gone ahead and booked one of the most expensive restaurants in town and was eager to fill me in on some exciting developments.

Having paid my rent, and most of my bills, I discover I have thirty-four cents left. Oh no. This can't be right. I have an important lunch on today. I am being wined and dined by a hugely successful producer whose support can alter the course of my life and put me back in the winners' circle. All these things race through my mind but still I'm looking at thirty-four cents. It's also now too late to cancel the lunch with some lame excuse. An excuse that doesn't fly could ruin what's left of your career. It'd have to be something really major like my leg fell off or something.

I keep staring at the coins in my hand hoping that by some miracle they'll multiply before my eyes. But they don't. God has chosen not to help as this is obviously a test of some sort. He has tested me so many times and I'm thinking I'd maybe like to drop out of whatever class I'm in.

Just then a friend phones me out of the blue and says he's going into the city. Oh yes there really is a God!

"Could you drop me off in the city?" I pleaded.

"Of course I can. What time do you have to be there?" he asks.

"No later than 12:30 p.m. A very powerful producer is taking me to lunch to talk about my project and if I'm late it could blow everything I've worked months ... years ... to build up."

"I'll be at your place at 11:45 a.m.!" he assures me.

"You promise?" I laugh nervously but am deadly serious.

"You know me."

Well, actually I do and you're always fucking late, I think to myself. But today I can't think negative thoughts. This lunch is meant to happen. It's my destiny. I can feel it.

I thank my friend profusely and hang up.

Next challenge – what clean clothes I have to wear? I try on a few combinations but the guy in the mirror looks like a clown on the make. I re-think things. Maybe the suit? Nah, he'll wear a suit and you don't want to look like it's a power play. After all, you're the creative guy. Creative people can get away with a lot, let's face it, they know we're crazy anyway. If we weren't why would we put up with this business? But normal people need the crazy creative. They pay us to look into the abyss and report back to them about what it's really like. They, who are too afraid to go to the edge, to look into the darkness (and have it look back into them), to unsettle their cozy lives in any way – have us. In the olden days there were court jesters to keep the king and his subjects amused. Today, the wealthy townsfolk know there's something scary out there in the dark so they send the crazies out to meet it and write a song or a book, or a play or a movie, or perhaps just act it out so the fat jolly ones with the perfect lives can feel a tingle of fear but know that it's only a movie and tomorrow is another day.

And they wonder why the creative drink, or take drugs, or fornicate to forget, or become John Galt and withdraw from this world all too soon.

I finally decide on the jeans, with loafers. I won't wear the boots as that'll make me taller than him and he may find that intimidating. Or just get plain pissed-off. Next the piece-de-resistance, the shirt. I go for the black with the fine grey line through it. Well, I mean it worked for Bob Dylan. Then again, that was thirty years ago. Too bad, it's the best I've got and I'm going with it. The black jacket tops it off nicely and I'm set. Oh, fuck look at my hair! It looks like a cross between Harpo Marx and Albert Einstein. Okay, off with the clothes and back into the shower to wash the hair again.

It's now 11:46 a.m. and my friend is late. He always gets annoyed when you question his punctuality – yet he is always late. So I wait. Perhaps I'll have my sixty-fourth coffee for the day? No, maybe not, as my hands are already shaking. Not a good look as people may think you're on meth or have that Katherine Hepburn disease.

It's midday and my friend is not here nor is he picking up his phone. Dread has set in and I'm overwhelmed with the feeling that I'm fucked. I torture myself by thinking of the wonderful life I could've had if only I hadn't let the most powerful producer in my universe sit alone at a restaurant. I'm done. It's over. I'm gone. All energy has left my body and I think I may go to bed and stay there forever. Or at least until I'm evicted. I wonder if there's a place they send creative when they've given up and get in the way of the revivalists taking their prized possessions to the tip? Could be worth researching but I don't have the energy. Why has God deserted me?

Suddenly I hear several frantic and loud beeps from a car outside. Thank you God! I love you! I'm on my feet again and energized with electricity. I lock the backdoor, not that there's anything to steal, and am off! My future awaits!

I get in the car and my friend who is graduate of the "Best Form of Defense Is Attack" berates me for keeping him waiting. But I don't have time for arguments, success calls me. I will deal with his tardiness sometime in the future, in the here and now, I am thrilled to be off and running.

The car doesn't start. Oh fuck God, why have you ...

"Don't worry, don't worry, it's been doing this all week. It's okay, calm down!" says my relaxed friend, who has absolutely no concept of time and motion. If I was in trauma I'd find him a fascinating character and someone I could use in a story sometime.

A few minutes' latter, the problem solved, we are on our way.

It's is now 12:25 p.m. and we are stuck in city traffic. The restaurant is several blocks away and I make the bold and desperate decision to bid my friend farewell, thank him, and jump from his car. I am now running through the city streets like a man gone mad. I realize the restaurant is all up hill. Maybe my decision was not well formed. This is confirmed when I see my friend drive past me with a look of "Are you nuts?"

Yes, I am nuts. And I have two minutes to be sitting at a table before the King who will wine and dine me and tell me whether I am to live or die. Or waste another year of my life. Not sure I have that many more to waste. You see, I always thought this world was a nice place to visit but was never really sold on wanting to live here.

I walk into the restaurant at 12:31 p.m. Actually, I heave into the restaurant as my lungs convulse trying to suck in enough air to sustain them. I am sweaty, the hair looks like I'm had an electrical shock, my lovely shirt is half hanging out and my jacket looks as tense as me. He is not here. The restaurant is empty and a lovely French girl hurriedly walks up to me and asks if I'd like some water. I'm sure she thinks I'm in the throes of a heart attack.

"No, I'm just in show business" I feel like saying but I don't have enough air in my lungs yet to force words out. She brings me a glass of water and I cradle it in my shaking hands and guzzle it down like some movie guy dying in the desert.

I give her the King's name and am escorted to a nice table for two. I sit alone and wait. That's really what this business is all about. Waiting. Those who don't die of boredom and give up, eventually win. If you live long enough, that is.

I am about to go to the bathroom and survey the damage the two-mile sprint has done to my appearance when the King arrives. I stand like a humble servant and greet him with all the respect a life that craves change can summon.

He is full of perfect teeth smiles, witty asides, showbiz gossip and ... the smell of success. I once knew that smell.

Right away he is down to business and demonstrating that he is indeed a man of action in a world of talk. But before he can elaborate, the waitress is upon us with menus and specials and wine lists and calculated grace. I wonder if her life is like mine or whether she has sold her dreams in order to pay the rent and buy some cheap food for her own table and cat. She looks like a cat person.

I am so engrossed in observing this girl, not in any sexual way, but with the eye of a writer, trying to look past her "act" and into her soul. I make up my mind that she is a good person and means me no harm. Such observations are important after a life like mine.

I look at the menu and am overwhelmed by the prices. And in my mind I remember back to the days when money was no object and I didn't even bother to check the cost of things. Why? There was so much money and so little time. I smile at the irony that those things have been reversed in my present life. Suddenly

I'm back at the Cannes Film Festival and dining at La Mere Besson, on the rue des Freres Pradignac, and life is good. I have a young son waiting for me at home and I've been on a spending spree buying him far too much, but tearful at how such things can't buy you time. I have finally succeeded in getting rid of my business partner (or so I think) and the company is now bouncing back better than ever. We have just screened my new movie "Flynn" starring Guy Pearce and Steven Berkoff and the sales agents can't keep up with the international bids on it.

Little did I know that these would be my last few days before the empire fell and my life would be altered for years. My son and I would also be casualties of that war brewing back home.

"Well, Frank, I think I may go with the duck pate."

I leave Cannes in my mind and am jolted back to the here and now. "Yes ... Yes ... that looks very nice. Let's make that two!"

"And for my main I'll order the rib eye medium rare," orders the King. The waitress scribbles the order and turns to smile at me.

I haven't even looked at all the menu items. I've been too busy at Cannes. Just in time I stop myself from telling them that there so many sales on my new film that the agents can't keep up with them. But I realize it's gone. It was all a dream that doesn't make sense or matter anymore.

I hear myself utter the word, "Gone." The waitress thinks this is her cue to refill my glass with water.

I order the rib eye too. Medium rare. I'm suddenly unable to make decisions. Y'see there were some decisions I made a long time ago that I thought would save the day, and people had their lives torn apart. Do you understand? But the waitress is gone too. And I'm beginning to think she has a dog at home and not a cat.

"Frank, I can't tell you how excited I am about your new play. It's going to be huge. I've also been talking to people in New York and there's no reason why we couldn't open it there in the fall of the 2017 season."

The fall of 2017? It's years away and I can't hold on any longer.

"You people are wasting my life," I tell them. "I have a son to feed ... no, to find ... and I have thirty-four cents in my pocket and I am naked and scared. I have given so much for so little in return and I've had enough."

I get up and look around. In some ways, seeing the place for the first time. "Where are you going?" asks the producer.

"I'm going to look at some new shirts. The one I'm wearing is tired of pretending it's something it's not. And so am I."

"But we have a meeting ... there's food coming ..."

I am now walking down the street and the sun on my face warms my soul. Just then I hear my young son's voice, "What's the matter Daddy? You look sad."

"No son, I'm good. Everything's just fine. I'm just a bit lost that's all. You know how scary it is when you get lost?"

Oliver laughs. "Don't worry, Daddy, it'll be alright when you grow up to be a child."

Then I feel his little hand in mine and he leads me down the hill. We get to the corner and as I'm about to turn left he stops me and says, "No ... no, Dad ... this is the way." And we turn right. And continue to walk in the sun.

Suddenly, reality hits and I stop.

"What's up, Dad?"

"I only have thirty-four cents. And that's not enough to get us home."

But he smiles at me with all the patience of a wise old soul and says, "But Dad, we're already home."

From God's POV, some of the people rushing to and fro on the busy street were annoyed that a stationary man, his arms outstretched to something only he could see, was in their way.

FH

{ 18 }

The Wounded Outnumber the Dead

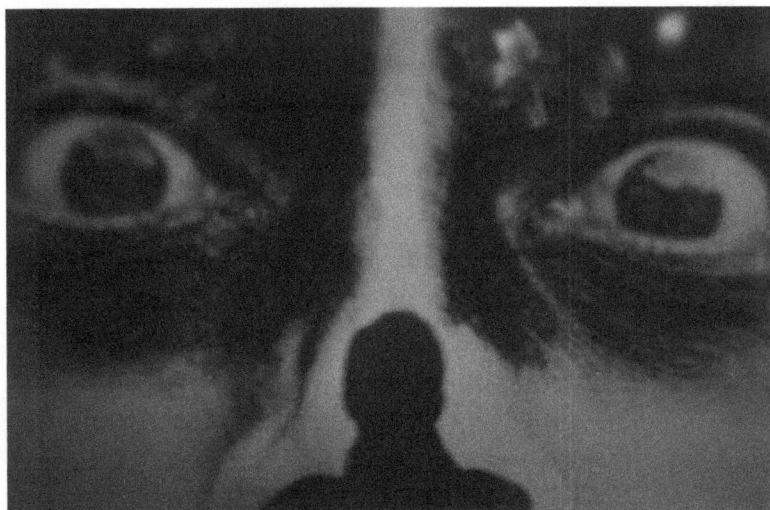

H owie Gordon looked out his tenth-story window at Beverly Hills below him. He observed the people rushing to and fro, or stuck in traffic on this Friday afternoon, and thought about how every one of them down there has a story. And they carry hope and hurt with them every day, and still try to function enough to make a living. It's a big balancing act for most of 'em and sometimes they topple over from the weight.

Howie was toppling but thankfully no one had noticed. Yet. For thirty-five years he had been one of the top agents in the movie industry and represented the who's who of anyone's dream list.

He had come up the hard way from the mail room boy, to gofer, to assistant, to whatever they threw at him. All the time watching and taking note of how the big guys worked. They all had one thing in common – they were obsessive. And generally rude unless it was someone they were trying to schmooze into leaving another agency for theirs, or lunching with a producer. As an agent your producer contacts and friends were your lifeblood.

It used to be one helluva ride. In those days he'd been fueled by a lust for power that was considered awesome by some, and frightening for the rest. No one got in Howie Gordon's way. He had blood on his hands and was old enough to see it. Maybe that's why he compulsively washed his hands every hour on the hour. He had killed many careers in his time. Squashed people out of existence over some slight that had offended him. Most times the imagined offender had no idea why his phone stopped ringing. Once you became "phone dead" in this town, it was all over. Sometimes you were the last to know.

Howie had been with some of the most beautiful and famous women in the world. Legends. Married a few of them too. He'd also balled all the prettiest young starlets that came through his office in search of a break. Howie was Number One so he got the cream of the crop. Some of them would do anything. He felt ashamed of some of the things he'd made these young women do. But it was as if he was fascinated to see how far someone would go before they lost themselves and everything they had been raised by. There weren't too many female stars that hadn't spent at least one night in his Benedict Canyon mansion. He could be very charming. Right up to the time he no longer took your calls.

Like most insatiable ladies' men, somewhere along the line he realized that it wasn't the sex act that was driving him on. It was about the conquest. It was about the ego. It was about him. He needed to be wanted. Desired. Adored. In his den he had thousands of deteriorating home videos of him performing sex acts on some of the most iconic actresses of his era. But he hadn't watched any of them in years. He hated movies.

Although he was not a religious man, he had heard a Biblical quote some years back, maybe in a movie, that now kept repeating in his head, "You are the salt of the earth; but if the salt has become tasteless, how can it be made salty again? It is no longer good for anything, except to be thrown out and trampled under foot by men."

He feared he had passed his use-by date and that people were too polite to tell him. He had anxiety attacks and took medication for them. He sometimes felt like he had stage fright when he went into a meeting. It made no sense. All of his life he'd had such control and now...he felt like he was coming apart. He took downers to go to sleep. He smoked meth to wake up. He took Viagra to fuck. He drank alcohol only because he'd done it so long now it was a habit. He smoked the occasional joint to relax. He took cocaine to feel normal. Well, to feel anything actually. He ordered meals in all the best restaurants and just stared at his plate. He was a man alone at the best table in the house.

"There goes Howie Gordon, he orders a $50 meal and leaves a $500 tip! And why? Because he can."

He often wondered if his life would be more tolerable if he'd had children. But then again, he'd always been so busy he would hardly have established a relationship with them. And now they'd be grown strangers. And who needed any more strangers in your life?

He only played golf because it was a good way to do business. He read scripts because he had to. He generally slept through movie screenings because everybody in the industry knew all the best ones had been made years ago.

He was finding it difficult to drive these days. His mind kept wandering and suddenly he'd be having conversations with ghosts from twenty years ago. Sometimes he'd catch himself as his car was veering across the line into oncoming traffic.

His thoughts were sometimes very dark and were filled with scenarios involving suicide and how best he could do it. Rather than frighten him, these imaginings gave him a sense of pleasure. Release. Comfort.

He always ended up at Santa Monica Beach at around midnight. One night the police had had to retrieve him from the dark water. He had wandered out into the darkness in his Armani suit and was just standing there breast deep in black water. Some guy who was cruising the beach saw him and called the cops.

He thought about Mary Krimshaw and wondered what had happened to her. She so believed in him. She had come to Hollywood to be a star and ended up in Howie's bed. The tragedy was she'd actually had the talent to achieve her dream but fell in with the wrong people. Well, with Howie. He often thought of her. Sometimes he felt she was the only one who'd ever really loved him. And he destroyed her. Tired of her. And passed her onto some producer friends who wasted her time too. Had he pimped out the only true thing in his life? Degraded it to something he could understand?

He could still see her bright, beautiful face and that smile that'd light up your life. She had been so young and full of hopes and dreams and vitality.

"I'm sorry, Mary ... I'm so sorry ..." he often mumbled in his office. Well, that's what his secretary thought he said.

Howie hated going into restaurants that he wasn't familiar with. Several times he'd been served by waitresses he recognized as starlets who could've made it only for him. One of them had been a breathtaking beauty in her prime and Howie became so guilt-stricken when he saw her that he emptied his wallet into her hand and left. He would've paid anything to get out of there. There were ghosts everywhere.

He often thought of Robert Wardling who could've been one of the great screenwriters but Howie resented his good looks and easy going charm, especially when it'd worked on a few of the same women he was seeing. It only took 12 phone calls to kill Wardling's career. But there you have it.

It was almost home time. Another Friday done, deadlines met, deals put to bed, careers stabilized. Howie told his secretary to book him his table at Dan Tana's for 9 p.m. That would give him time to drive home, have a scotch on ice by the swimming pool he'd never entered, a bath, dress, a gram of the finest cocaine and sit at Dan Tana's staring into another beautiful meal that would go untouched.

"The salt is tasteless ..." he muttered to himself as an attentive waiter replaced the salt shaker and apologized.

The great Howie Gordon looked over at the bar and several attractive women smiled at him. They either knew who he was or were hookers smelling a well-heeled john. But it didn't matter anymore. Life had as little meaning to him as the last couple of movies he'd had to stay awake through to please a client.

He wondered what Mary Krimshaw was doing tonight. And where. For all he knew she may be dead. As dead as him.

A little after midnight, Howie Gordon opened the drawer of his bedside table, took his Smith and Wesson snub-nosed pistol and placed a bullet in his temple. Then everything went to black. Just like a movie did at the end before the credits rolled.

Hollywood was in shock when the news broke. There was the usual outpouring of gushy love, glowing obits and tribute pieces. Another of the greats had gone was the feeling of the day. No one could understand why a man who had everything would take his own life.

Somewhere in Ohio, a hotel receptionist by the name of Mary Krimshaw cried.

{ 19 }

The Interrogation of John Doe

Once, I was arrested and interrogated about things I didn't know. Now I make sure I look more closely at things. You never know when you'll be forced to testify. Did you know that the origin of the word "testify" is from the old Roman court which required men to swear on their testicles that they were telling the truth?

No?

Anyway, my run-in with the law was years ago, but they continue to interrogate me using more sophisticated weapons and devices. They must think I'm stupid.

It can be exhausting searching the house every night for bugs and hidden cameras but it must be done. If I can't find them I make sure I sit at home and say things out loud that I don't really mean like, "I love the government and all it stands for" or "It would be a good time to plant cherries."

I try to be seen only ever drinking water.

If I read, I make sure I'm seen with the book "Thoughtful Things To Do With Your Life" by Malcolm Fraser. It is actually only the cover and it hides my true reading matter, "How To Make A Bomb And Impress A Large Amount of People."

Sometimes the tap drips but I let it. I want whoever's watching to know I'm very patient.

At night I hear footsteps in my kitchen but I stay in bed. Early in the morning the sound of a woman showering and clearing her nose. Well I think that's what she's doing. I'm afraid to confront her in case we haggle about her paying rent so I just let her go about her business of doing nothing and staying out of my way.

I used to lock the doors till I realized I may in fact not be locking these people out, but in. That unnerved me and I took myself to bed for a few months.

I no longer buy the morning newspaper because I once caught it looking at me.

I may be wrong but my coffee tastes strange. I now only pretend to drink it in case I raise suspicions.

The television is full of hidden meanings so I tune out. It once told me the world was in a pretty good place. That's when I knew it was lying.

When I was arrested they asked me my name but I didn't tell them. Then they tortured me by bringing up my family. I asked to go to the toilet and tried to drown myself in the bowl.

I told them I was innocent but they said "everyone tells us that! Tell us something we don't know."

So I told them, "The reason firehouses have circular stairways is because in the old days the engines were pulled by horses. The horses were stabled on the ground floor and figured out how to walk up straight staircases."

They beat me until I bled for that one.

They asked me what I knew about the KGB. I told them that the letters KGB stand for Komitet Gosudarstvennoy Bezopasnosti. I got another beating for that. Then they said they'd give me one last chance to tell them something they wanted to hear.

So I thought I'd hit 'em with the big one. The one that never failed to impress the circle I mixed in. "Emus and kangaroos cannot walk backwards and are on the Australian coat of arms for that reason."

They jumped on my head. I was rushed to hospital and a full recovery but sometimes I think I haven't been the same. But I forget.

{ 20 }

The Ghost of Alister Holmes

T he old man was dying. He'd been aware of it for some time now. He just knew it. He had exhausted himself on so many dreams and people and somehow had never been replenished by finding that special someone who makes it all seem worthwhile.

Alister Holmes was only 62 but felt a thousand. Like Scott Fitzgerald he believed that it was possible to become an emotional bankrupt.

These days, and nights, he walked the streets and haunted the places that had once meant something to him. This was the whole world as he knew it now. Some people believe you have to die to become a ghost but Alister knew better. His only company, now, were other ghosts. He'd sit in the park where his father used to take him as a child and he'd talk out loud to him. And in his head his father would respond. He couldn't help thinking that death had mellowed his father tremendously. These days Dad mostly agreed with his son about everything. He knew better than to tell this to anyone lest they think he was insane.

Sometimes, if he was extra sentimental, he'd stand outside the little weatherboard house he'd been brought up in and chat with his mother. Passersby would stare but he was too old to give a fuck. He thought about his Uncle Horrie and how everyone had always seemed nervous and on edge when his uncle was around. Even though Alister was a just kid at the time he'd noticed how Uncle Horrie always tried too hard for a laugh, an acknowledgement, a smile, anything. The poor man never seemed to be at ease, which probably explained the chain smoking that took him to an early grave. He died alone, in hospital.

"Why hadn't we all gone to visit him? He'd loved us didn't he?" Alister asked his mother without ever receiving a sensible reply.

Then years later he found out that his Uncle Horrie had actually been his eldest brother. His mother had been raped when she was 14 and Horrie was the result. The poor bastard became the living embodiment of a horror and shame and scandal. Both he and his mother were innocent victims but they paid the price and dealt with it badly in their own ways. Horrie hated his name Horrie or Horace so he insisted on correcting everyone and telling them that his name now was Jim. Everyone'd nod dutifully and then after two drinks forget and continue to call him Horrie. Then Horrie, or Jim, would get upset and storm out. Alister sometimes would tear up when he'd think of how humiliated this man must've felt being disowned within his own family. Never being listened to, never been acknowledged as a whole person. Horrie had prematurely experienced what it was like to be a ghost too. Alister liked to believe there was a heaven and that the two of them, mother and son, are now together and at peace. No more shame. No more dirty little secrets that damaged innocent lives. In the end it must all fall away, surely? What does it matter anymore? There can be no bigger picture than eternity.

Alister Holmes knew he carried some of his mother's stubbornness in him, as well as her capacity for love, and life had been a constant battle as to which side would win at any given problem. But he had tried, he surely had, and in trying had come the weariness that was now overtaking him. He had joked that his downfall had been his liking for people. So many of them had gotten the better of him and diminished him in spirit and in heart. But for the thousands he'd befriended it'd been worth it for the handful of friends he'd found. A few who were loyal enough to not have a negative word said about you in their presence. Such friends were as rare as hen's teeth in these times of gossip, backstabbing and elevation at another's expense, but they did exist.

Alister smiled when he thought of those dear friends he'd been lucky enough to find. Some were no longer of this world and had joined the passing parade on the other side. But he did continue to chat with them every day. He was a loyal friend if nothing else, and he never forgot a kind gesture and a true heart. His day would usually end down by the beach watching the sunset. He found it puzzling, and fascinating, that God finally grants us wisdom just as the light is ebbing. Why? So we can look back at our lives and understand all the mistakes we made? Perhaps that is the true hell. It is not a place, it is a feeling. And once we have acknowledged it, truthfully, we are released to experience the bliss of letting go.

Alister had walked away so much of his life in dark deserted alleys. Sometimes, filled with a joy bordering on euphoric and, because he had no one to share it with, he'd walk it away until he was so utterly exhausted he could then go home and sleep. Perhaps that was the greatest metaphor of what Life really is. We come into it alone, our greatest despair and happiness usually experienced alone, and then of course, the final mystery revealed alone. Alister was dying and it wouldn't be long now.

He knew that.

People were coming back into his life as if it was choreographed that they should say goodbye and have one last hug. He had no regrets and seemed at peace. He'd been weary for some time and spent most of his energy trying to cover it with a smile. He knew they'd be surprised when he was gone. He'd given no indication and had covered his tracks well. He hoped to hell this was his last life and that he wouldn't be back. He felt he'd pretty much said it all this time around. God had equally blessed him as well as cursed him on this final ride through and perhaps that's what comes at the end.

You get to experience the whole giddy carnival in all the glory and tackiness befitting a finale. Just as the sun was sinking into the water, the only thing that sprang to his mind were the words that George M. Cohan would say at the end of each show he starred in, "My mother thanks you, my father thanks you, my sisters thank you, and as for me ... well that goes without saying."

{ 21 }

Shek-O Beach

It had been 50 years since Bill Cassell had set foot on Shek-O Beach in Hong Kong. He was still a young man when he'd walked onto these sands all those years ago. Although well preserved he'd lost along the way all those things that define you as a young man – ambitions, dreams, hope, confidence and the infinite belief that everything would work out for the best. Now he stood on this empty beach clinging to his last remaining hope. A hope so thin and futile he felt ashamed at how pathetic he'd become in his old age.

50 years ago on this beach he'd been stopped by a young Chinese girl selling hats. He'd looked at her and everything had changed. It wasn't just her obvious beauty, there was something else about her – perhaps her calmness, perhaps the wisdom in her twinkling eyes, her joyous laugh, the feeling that he meant something to her – that suggested there could be a purpose in his meandering and confused life. He'd bought the hat he didn't need and they'd chatted. They'd also laughed and enjoyed each other's company for what may've only been 10 minutes in total, and then she'd bid him farewell and walked away. But had never left him. He'd promised to come back and see her tomorrow but his Aussie buddies had gotten him drunk that night and he slept all the next day, nearly missing his night time flight back home. Since the encounter there'd not been a day when he hadn't thought of her and wondered how she was. He hoped maybe she'd thought of him too. Such are the dreams that torment old men.

Where had 50 years gone? Oh that's right, he'd returned to Australia, and married a safe convenient woman approved by everyone as a "good catch" and had then worked his guts out to buy a home to make sure his marriage remained safe and convenient. Then children had come along and gone. And finally, so had his wife, taking the safe and convenient home with her. He was now standing on the beach at Shek-O a laughing stock to his own logic but he was too old to care anymore. And it was almost dark.

How come 10 minutes had meant so much in his life and 50 years hadn't? Perhaps it's one of the cruel jokes God plays on us. Penalizing us for not following our instincts and wasting our lives in safety. Surely He gave us a life to live, not to hide in. Bill had discovered this wisdom all too late and it was in the knowing that the severest pain comes.

He asked some of the bar people overlooking the beach whether they remembered her. But most couldn't understand him. In the nearby village a wise looking old Chinese medicine man listened patiently to Bill's story all the while looking intently into his sad eyes. Bill guessed he too couldn't understand a word and was trying to decipher meaning by other means. When Bill was finished his manic raving, the old Chinese medicine man smiled and nodded his head. Maybe he was used to silly old Western men retracing their bad decisions and too kind to tell the latest lost soul that it was gone. Gone, gone, gone.

Bill walked back to the beach as if it might miraculously manifest her. And there he stood for hours until it was night. He did the same thing the next day and then next day. His skin was burned red by the lack of a sun hat. Or someone caring enough to offer him one. By the third day some locals had gathered to watch this strange man pacing up and down the length of the beach, fully clothed.

So many thoughts stampeded through Bill's mind. The years he'd lived up to those blissful 10 minutes and all the wasted time he'd spent in its shadow. Perhaps God gives us the opportunity for happiness and leaves it to us to recognize its face when we see it. Unfortunately, when we make the wrong decisions we spend the rest of our lives cursing him, like a spoiled child who didn't get what he wanted for Christmas.

A curious old local lady spectator to this dilemma asked the Chinese medicine man to explain what was happening. And in his Mandarin tongue he answered, "If you hold onto some dreams too long they damn you to hell."

The old Chinese lady looked back at that stranger on the beach as if she vaguely understood. She'd once sold sun hats there and had waited for weeks for a boy to return and be her friend. He'd seemed like such a nice person. And was so full of enthusiasm and dreams. But she was wise enough to know that it'd been in another life, or so it seemed.

On the beach, Bill Cassell paced ceaselessly, searching for his youth and driven mad by longing. Trapped in the hell of his own making. And ranting at the deserting tide.

{ 22 }

Christmas In St. Kilda

Harry Grivens had inherited it from his mother. An obsessive excitement about all things Christmas. His mother, Mary, would start her Christmas shopping January every year, her secret way of accruing all the magical gifts that dwarfed her illuminated pine tree every 25th of December. From her meagre budget she miraculously produced gifts for her children, her husband, her relatives, friends, and even homeless people she had struck up conversations with on the street.

Harry always said he'd found the spirit of Christmas in her eyes, which brimmed with tears of joy as she handed out her gifts to each and every one. He called her Mary Christmas.

Now here he was, a boy grown into a man, an old man, rushing around his little rented apartment with all the enthusiasm of his youth. It was dawn of Christmas morn and all his gifts for those nearest and dearest to him surrounded his little electronic tree in the living room. As he manically prepared the turkey, roasted the chicken, and cut the ham into generous slices, he wondered who'd be the first to show up at his door. Everyone had accepted his invitation with such surprise and enthusiasm that he laughed wondering how his little apartment would hold them all. He knew somewhere, in that other country, that thinly veiled dimension, his Mum was smiling at him and proud of the efforts he'd made to duplicate her day of giving.

He was betting that his son, Jamie, would be the first to excitedly knock on his door. Harry hadn't spent a Christmas with him in eighteen years. He stopped carving the ham as he froze in the stunted memory of where all those years had gone. A tear appeared in his eye as he thought about what a wonderful Christmas gift it'd be if God gave him back all those years. He had made so many mistakes. Not out of meanness or not caring but just because so much had happened 18 years ago to pull the rug out from under his established life that he'd had no experience in how to think straight in such circumstances. His successful and envied life had come to an abrupt end at the peak of his ability when he ended his partnership with a man he no longer trusted and who seemed hell-bent on self-destructing, taking all those who rode with him along for the nosedive. Harry had thought he was doing the noble thing by getting rid of this man. Yes, he was standing up over a principle and although he didn't expect to be lauded a hero, he certainly hadn't anticipated the trauma and devastation that awaited him and those he'd loved.

He looked down at the cold wet sensation of his finger and realized he'd cut himself with the carving knife. He hadn't even felt it. Perhaps he was numb to everything when he thought of those wasted years. Perhaps his only way of dealing with the loss. His business partner fine-printed Harry out of his fortune and assets until he had nothing but his integrity left. But Harry was to learn that such a high moral ideal meant nothing to anyone if you had no money and a tarnished reputation by association. They judged winners by who got away with the most money. Harry realized he'd have to wait for a much higher judgment if he wanted an acknowledgment for doing the right thing.

Harry unsteadily sat on the nearest chair and looked down at the blood dripping from his hand. He thought of Pontius Pilate washing the blood from his hands rather than making a decision to save the life of another: and Pilate's terse remark to Jesus when the prisoner mentioned truth, "What is truth? Your truth or mine?" Harry's body started to jerk uncontrollably now as he bowed his head and sobbed for the naïve, good man he once had been. After eighteen years in the wilderness Harry strongly doubted that he'd ever stand up over a principle again. He couldn't afford to. Everything was gone you see? The work, the money, the house, the marriage, the child whom he'd loved more than life itself, and, now, finally Harry. Looking down at the pool of blood at his feet he realized how deep the cut was and knew he was bleeding to death. The blood was draining from his body and he was feeling weak. Numb. Even more numb than usual. The thought of that ignited something in him and he rose and kicked the chair into the next room narrowly missing breaking many of the gift wrapped presents piled high around his $13.99 electric Christmas tree. He grabbed a napkin from the table and pressed it down hard against the wound. He turned off the oven, made it down the stairs and hailed a taxi to the ER of his nearest hospital.

When the nurse on duty saw the blood-soaked napkin Harry was immediately admitted deemed unsuitable for waiting. He was rushed into a room where a nice Indian doctor sowed up his cut and made jokes that Harry laughed at without really hearing. He was concerned, no, distressed, that his son may've shown up at his door to find him not home. And that he'd think his father had let him down again. He wanted him to know that he didn't do these things on purpose and that some things are beyond your control. They just … happen. They just happen. The kindly doctor, aware of Harry's anxiety and, to him, incoherent rambling about his son, administered a sedative and had a nurse escort his patient to an outside cab rank.

As Harry climbed the stairs to his apartment his inherited Christmas spirits rose again and he found himself calling out, "Jamie are you there? Here I come! I had a stupid accident that's all … you know me! Accident prone … Your silly Dad, huh? Don't worry, just give me an hour and you'll have the feast of your life!"

But reaching the top floor he realized he was talking to himself. He looked down in hope to see if there were any tell tale signs that his son had come, waited, and gone. But no. There'd been no visitors from what he saw. None at all.

With some difficulty he inserted the key into his lock and opened the front door. He was home. Whatever that meant. A new enthusiasm energized him when he looked at the clock and realized it was still only 10:30 a.m. What an idiot he was. His guests hadn't arrived yet because it hadn't reached the appointed hour. Hope sprang eternal again. He turned on the oven again and looked around at all his preparations and felt the joy his mother had felt all those years ago, knowing what a wonderful day awaited the cherished ones.

At 2:45 p.m. Harry found himself sitting at the head of his small table, wearing his Christmas hat, and staring at the perfectly roasted turkey, chicken, sliced ham, rustic potatoes and other goodies worthy of a king on a budget. In the background Christmas music played on endless repeat and now he was listening to Bing Crosby, his Mum's favourite. He turned off the pot of boiling water bringing life to his plum pudding and caught a reflection of himself in the shiny salt and pepper shakers. He looked ridiculous. He wearily took his Christmas hat off and went to sit in his living room to gaze at all the unopened gifts.

He'd been hoping to have a beautiful bonding Christmas day with his son which explained his anxiousness about every detail of it being perfect. He'd wanted him to experience the type of Christmas his dad had known when he was young, and his mother was still alive.

Harry's ex-wife had not allowed their son to spend one Christmas day with his dad in eighteen years and even when Harry had gone to a woman lawyer, who was appalled at the situation and sent Harry's ex several very serious legal letters, Jamie's mother defused the situation by agreeing to allow Harry and son a Christmas. But unlike Christmas, it never came. There was always a reason. Harry wondered how someone could hurt another so cruelly. Had he treated her so? Or was she just bitter that the money and the expensive trinkets all went away?

She had also told his son lies. Told him Harry had deserted them both. Left them with nothing. Never paid alimony. Lies, lies, lies. Trouble was, how could Harry set the record straight without telling his son his mother was a liar? He'd attempted to explain the real story one day but it ended bitterly with another two precious years wasted in not talking.

The truth was that eighteen years ago Harry's career had finished in his homeland. Although he'd taken action to get rid of his business partner, those facts were buried deep beneath the guilty by association tag that was so much easier for people to remember. In the end he was advised by his lawyer, friends and wife that it'd be easier to resume his career in Los Angeles where he was still highly regarded. Over there the only thing that lived was the work, not the innuendo and cocktail gossip. In fact, his wife, so convinced it was the right decision, eagerly drove him to the airport. He'd realized later that she'd wanted him gone as she had a more promising option awaiting his exit. Harry had left her everything his business partner hadn't taken, mainly a big mansion and everything in it. The sale of it intended as a big one lump sum payment to her and the welfare of their son. In contrast, Harry walked through the airport departure door with a suitcase, the clothes he was wearing and enough money to last him a year in L.A if he lived like a monk. Then one year became two, then three and so on for nine years that seemed to go by like nine months.

Harry sat on his couch and thought that perhaps he deserved this Christmas. He couldn't wait until New Year's Eve to pledge that he would never stand up over a principle again; or love something too much lest it be taken from you.

His only ambition now was a simple one – he just wanted his son to know the truth and how much his dad had loved him, and … everything.

Then he looked up and saw his mother standing by the electronic flashing Christmas tree. Her eyes were filled with that all too familiar Christmas joy and her accompanying smile not only warmed Harry's heart but healed it.

"Have you been a good boy, son?"

"Yes Mum, I have tried so hard to be. But I feel old and weary from the trying."

"What do you want most this Christmas, Harry? And I'll see if I have it for you."

Harry's voice trembled as it always did when he got too emotional, "I want to be home, Mum. I've been trying to get back there for so long but I think I took the long way. And got lost somewhere."

Harry felt something and realized his wound had reopened. Maybe they all have to be reopened before one can truly begin again?

No one was in Harry's apartment to see him go. So many had wanted to be there but things just got in their way. But that was Life, huh?

Part Two: Essays & Other Bruises

Writing in Restaurants

t's nice to find those restaurants where you become part of the furniture and they accept that you're an eccentric that just sits for hours and looks into thin air smiling, or eyes welling with tears, before jotting your thoughts, memories or visions down in your trusty notebook. A notebook that looks as though it has done as many miles as its owner. They clear away your plates and refill your coffee and leave you in peace to reimagine your life and what has been, or imagine the future and the ever fading promise you cling to.

You observe everything. It's part of your job. There is no such thing as the unintentional gesture or the frivolous conversation overheard at a nearby table. It all means something to you because your role in life is to look for meaning in everything. Maybe it's your way of trying to make sense of things or make up for a childhood that was so chaotic it was difficult to grasp onto much.

As I once remarked to P.F. Sloan, in a restaurant, "That's why they pay us. We are the freaks that normal folk send to the abyss to look into it and report back to them about the horror. Or worse, the nothingness that is

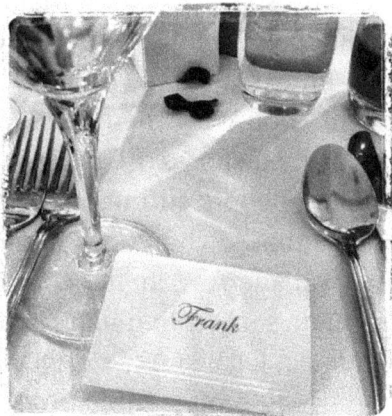

found at the end of the rainbow." But I guess dear Judy found that out for herself.

You have been made strong by every hurt your heart has endured. Yet the simplest things can still reduce you to tears. That is your curse. You care too much and always have. It is your greatest gift and your greatest affliction. But there is no rehab for it. And try as much as you do to pretend that you don't give a damn, the truth is you do.

One of the things that gets to you is the sight of young lovers dining together at a table for two. They hold hands because they can't bear to not touch each other. It's so sweet that it makes your eyes water in spite of yourself. You wonder what their story is and what the harsh future holds for them. But you want them to be Alright. You want them to make it. In fact, you might even write a story where they survive it all and still end up as old people sitting on a park bench holding hands. Perhaps that's why you became a writer so you could play God and rewrite the ending until it was something that made sense. So much in life only makes sense from a distance. Or when it's done.

You see the table of businessmen making deals. Each one conning the other, distorting the facts, bragging about their toys and their women, and yet naïve enough to think they're going to get away scott free. Little do they know that each lie they tell will be a year of their life lost to regret and confusion somewhere down the line. Like that train a'comin' in "High Noon" every action will one day have to be faced. Not in hell, that would be too easy, but in life.

You drink coffee like it's water. You have nerves of caffeine but it sharpens the brain so that you don't miss anything; the waiter's smile; the wife who steals a look at another man sitting alone; the businessman who hides a yawn behind his hand as the man sitting opposite him is just getting warmed up with his pitch. The "pitcher" so wants to be able to go home tonight and tell his wife he's a hero. That he has saved their day. That he has pulled off the deal of the century and their future is assured. He longs to have his wife look at him again with love in her eyes instead of the disappointment that has beaten them both down holding onto this damn dream. Perhaps, like Willy Loman, it was the wrong dream and the right one passed them by unnoticed. He is not sure how many more meetings he can take without screaming at someone to truly listen to him.

I put my pen away and close the book. I finish my coffee and pay the bill. I wander home amongst the throng of people going to and fro and try to shut my mind off. I can't tell everyone's story. Instead I think about dinner and whether it is worth cooking a meal for one. Cooking is therapeutic. Like golf, it requires that you shut everything else out except the matter at hand. I like it. It calms and focusses me. Once there was a big table and a room filled with laughter and love. Everyone loved the atmosphere of our home and they'd all just call in unannounced because they knew no one would be turned away and that there was always enough wine and food and a big open fire. And in our home they would feel at home. But that's another story and too painful to write or even think about.

* * *

Finding Your Voice

Learn everything you can
Then forget it
The thing that makes you unique as a person
Is the very thing that will make your art
original
Protect your own point of view
It's all we have
To separate us
From the journeymen and the hacks
Many will tempt you with compromises

Promises of
rewards
And attempt to kill
you
With fake praise
It will not be easy
to resist seduction
But when was
anything worth
achieving
Easy?
Tell your stories
Your way
And as long as there is truth
At the heart of them
People will respond
We live in a world where the public seldom get
to see
Or hear the truth
So if you tell your story
with honesty
And don't cloud it with phony "how to write a

saleable script' formulas
and performances that don't ring true
You have a chance to make a mark
Don't let your craven need for ego-driven
success
Get in the way of your destination
Those who are only in it for the money
Or the praise
Or the girls
Or the boys
Or the parties
Or the power
May get what they want
But they won't be remembered
Concentrate on one thing
And one thing only
Do great work
Work that makes you proud
That, in itself, is its own reward
Be true to your gift
Lest it be taken from you
Like anything it needs to be nurtured
And respected by oneself
Once you sell your integrity
You don't get it back
Harden everything but your heart
To the slings of ridicule and belittlement
In some circles, sadly, you will measure your
success
By the level of resentment that targets you
Ignore the praise and the criticism
Both are liars
Designed to derail your work and journey
Critics write from the head
You write from the guts

You are probably destined to never understand
each other
I have lived
And worked
and battled
Won
And lost
in the fields of wonder
And won again
I am the old guard now
A weary soldier that hopefully made
Some headway or impression
For those outsiders or mavericks that follow
But as I look around
My heart is warmed
By you
The young
The gifted
and the brave
and no one is more proud of your achievements
Than I
For you are the future
What you make today
Becomes the legacy for tomorrow
And those that will follow you
I salute you
I honour you
And I respect your commitment
And guts to go forward
Give nothing but the best of yourself
Don't let the system make you feel ashamed
For being original
Or being truthful
Or being you
There is no one like you in the world

We are all unique
Let that be reflected in your work
Yes, find your own voice
And don't let anyone take it from you
Life is a long time to live with regret
Believe in yourself
As much as I believe in you.

(Speech delivered at the 15th. Melbourne
Underground Film Festival opening.)

* * *

Life of the Artist

It's a Spartan life. Simple days amidst the complexities
of Art. You will learn to observe everything because
you're always in search of
material and the next
inspiration.

    You will see
pretenders drive past you in
limousines on their way
home to mansions, but don't
be envious of the poor in
spirit. Their hardships will
come in other areas. No one
gets out of this life without
scars of some kind.

    When the money
comes you will be generous to a fault, but when it
doesn't you will live like a monk. That will give you the

gift of solitude and reflection that will enlighten your work. Sometimes you will feel like a machine. A pulsating, deeply caring but hurt, piece of machinery put on this earth to soak up all the follies and foibles of a world gone mad and to print out the pages of your observations and feelings about it.

Do not work for those who do not either understand or appreciate the process. If you do it will leave you confused and broken hearted. It brings rust to the machine. And you are too poor and too old for repairs.

Drink and laugh with real friends because that is what renews you. It is far better to laugh at the world than to cry over it.

You may not be fully appreciated during your own life. That is a cruel reality that takes some accepting. But die with the knowledge that if you have done your job well and, if some kind advocates preserve it, it will live on. And thus so will you.

Die with your boots on. Keep working no matter what. It's what you were put here to do. It is your gift and your curse.

Always feed the child within you. It's nice to have experienced many things and to intellectualize about them, but it is the child within you that will always cut to the truth of any situation. Sometimes speaking out of turn.

Love the few, but appreciate the many.

There are those who will resent your gift and work against you. Pity them for they are starving. But do not feed them.

Life is a circus and you have been bred to perform in the ring. It will take guts to swallow the fear and to lose/find yourself within that spotlight. The weight of that glow will break some. Many in fact. Those who stand their ground will grow roots.

All the most beautiful things in the world have developed the strength to survive. Some are protected by thorns.

* * *

Bob Dylan

Like all great things, Bob Dylan is an acquired taste. Some people don't like caviar. Others will pay a fortune for it. Who is right? No one. You get out of it what you need, or you don't at all. And that is cool. In the words of Dylan, "it's all good."

One of the most frustrating things about Art is none of us can agree about it. Look at the critics. They can't even agree. You read some reviews about yourself and you've failed magnificently. You pick up another paper to read that you're a genius. And again, who's right? The truth is neither of them. What it is is what it is to each individual person based upon their own personal life experience. Some people can stand in front of the Mona Lisa and feel nothing. I say time is the

only true judge of something's worth. And after 50 years and at 75 years of age Bob Dylan is still going, God bless him, and we are all the better for it.

It always intrigues me when someone goes to a Dylan show and says "He didn't perform he just stood there, or sat at the keyboards, and sang the songs." Well, that's all he's ever done. Even when he burst onto the scene like a meteorite, he just stood at the microphone and played his songs on guitar and sang, with a shyness most of us found endearing. Like he was singing something so personal it was too revealing even to himself.

He now says those early songs he must've channeled from a higher being because he doesn't know where they came from. And even he remains startled by some of the things that young boy wrote. "They had a magic to them. I can't do that anymore. I do something else now." The magic has been replaced by craftsmanship. And what a craftsman he is.

There are those who say they hate his voice and he can't sing. Well, which voice are they referring to? He's had about six different voices over the journey. You want to hear a pleasant voice that is an instrument? Go see Tony Bennett next time he comes to town.

Some people have voices that are technically brilliant, and I'm in awe of their gift. But after a few songs I find my mind wandering and it all becomes a bit boring. Just my personal opinion. I think that's why I've always gravitated to the originals. People who sing with individuality. Perhaps it's called passion. As Don McLean described Dylan in "American Pie" he sang in "... a voice that came from you and me." And that voice sang songs about losers, drifters, hobos, dust bowl survivors, slaves, forgotten blues singers, Jewish prophets, misunderstood gangsters, a lawman who became Judas to his best friend, people who'd been shut out of society because of the colour of their skin, and men who'd been wrongly imprisoned for things they hadn't done. His voice was their voice.

I one day played my son the song "Hurricane" about the travesty, or the pig-circus of justice that convicted Rubin "Hurricane" Carter to many years in jail and a nightmare he couldn't wake from. I told my son, "Bob cared so much about this man that he wrote this song and the reaction to it led to a retrial for Rubin and his eventual release." My son, Oliver, a wise old soul, looked at me and said, "But Dad, Bob cares about everyone. Don't you listen to his lyrics?"

I told that story to P.F. Sloan, who'd known Bob for many years, and P.F looked at me, smiled and said, "Oliver got that right."

In many ways I think Bob's gift has been a huge burden to him. At the heart I think he's a shy, very sensitive man, and the fanaticism surrounding him embarrasses and probably sometimes angers him that it's made him a prisoner. He once said, in answer to a question about why at his age he still tours, "The only time I know who I am is when I'm onstage."

Many creative people know what that is like. It's like we weren't given this life for our own enjoyment, but rather to serve the gift. And this gift has taken us from our loved ones, our home, and the wheels that drive a normal life.

When I was young I was very shy, some find this hard to believe, but I learnt how to push through that. Or perhaps you get to an age where you don't give a fuck what others think of you and with that comes a great relief. A liberation. In my younger days I could easily perform to 2,000 people but was far more nervous having a one-to-one conversation with anyone. That is the ultimate contradiction of most performers.

I also love and admire Bob's bravery. His guts to follow his own instincts without an eye on the box office or the record charts or even what his fans want him to do. To me that is a true artist. That boldness and commitment to follow your gift's course at the expense of your own comfort and career safety.

There is a lovely and very revealing story about the young Bob Dylan. He was one of the few great artists of his time that didn't perform on the Ed Sullivan Show, although he'd been booked to do it. He got as far as the rehearsal for the show and sang a new song, "The John Birch Society Blues," a song about America's paranoia of communists. He performed the new tune and the producer of the show came down from the control room and told Bob that the song was unacceptable for prime time viewing in America, and that Bob should do "Blowin' In The Wind" instead. Bob went to his dressing room and thought about how his parents and all his uncles and aunts were excitedly gathered around the TV set in Minnesota awaiting his appearance on the Ed Sullivan Show. They were so proud of him. He then made a decision that would define the rest of his career. He put his guitar into his guitar case, put on his jacket, and quietly walked out of the TV studio onto the winter streets of New York and went home. What a huge decision for a young boy to make, and yet that decision determined who he was going to be. If he'd compromised then, how could he not compromise again in the future? Once you sell your integrity you don't get it back.

I love Bob. He has inspired me most of my life. And like any bold artist he is not afraid of trying something and being laughed at. In fact, there were many times in the '80s when he was laughed at and, even more cruelly, dismissed as no longer relevant. But he stuck to his course and has, over the last 15 years, made one of the most stunning and unexpected comebacks in show business scoring three Number One albums, more than he'd had in his supposed heyday.

So many of the great ones are gone. And so sadly missed. Imagine, no pun intended, just what John Lennon may've done over the past 30 years. We are so blessed that Bob is still with us. And still bravely evolving, going where others are too scared or compromised to tread.

Long may you reign, Bobby.

* * *

Thoughts On Robin Williams

It was always his eyes that got to me. No matter how hard he smiled or how manic his brain was working, machine-gunning out hysterical one-liners, most of which you missed because you were too busy laughing at the last one – his eyes were sad. The sadness of a man who possibly knew that the world was insane and he was just going to go with it.

To me all the great comedians have one thing in common – they see the world from a unique point-of-view. Sometimes it's not even that the one liners are that funny. What is humorous is their perspective on things. They see the bizarre in the things we take for granted, the mundane actions we mostly do on auto-pilot without even thinking about. But they do.

Another great example of this humour is Ricky Gervais. We identify and laugh at how silly and futile some of the things we do and say really are under the light of scrutiny.

I know a woman who worked for a TV show in Los Angeles for some time and she said one of the many guest stars on the show over the years had been Robin Williams. She told me when he arrived he was with rigid with nerves. He was concerned he wouldn't be funny. He was intimidated by the guest star on the previous week's show and that he couldn't top what they'd done, etc., etc., etc. She said he got so worked up he almost walked out before the taping and she had to calm him down and assure him he'd be wonderful. Perhaps that explains his rapid fire delivery of one-liners. They were being propelled at us from the nervousness he felt inside. What a drain that must've been on him and how exhausted he must've felt after every show, like a champion boxer after every title bout. Ironically, that inner fear that ate him away like a cancer also made him great.

That is the way with many great artists. Their flaws or perceived disabilities are their strengths.

Having spent many years researching the life of Bobby Darin for a new musical I have written, I was struck by a comment from his son, Dodd. He said that the heart problem that had afflicted his father from an early age also propelled him to greatness. Bobby had overheard a doctor say to his mother, "If that kid lives to sixteen it'll be a miracle." Now, there are two ways you can go with that knowledge. Either you just give up and think what's the use of doing anything or you can go the other way and squeeze everything you can into every minute you have left. Dodd Darin has said, "People think that disease killed my father. Oh no, it made my father."

Robin Williams said he was once advised to go see a shrink. He made the appointment and went to the therapist, laid down on his couch and talked about his life and his problems. At the end of it, the therapist said to him, "I think I can cure you, but you may not be funny anymore." Robin got up, shook hands with the guy and left never to return. The world thanks him for that decision but damn, what a burden he carried for our pleasure.

Like you I will miss Robin Williams not being in the world. His absence, like that of John Lennon, makes all our lives a little colder. All I know is I'm going to miss him for a long, long time.

Every time I hear Smokey Robinson and the Miracles sing "Tracks of my Tears" I will think of him, "... So take a good look at my face, you'll see my smile looks out of place, if you look closer it's easy to trace the tracks of my tears."

Rest in peace, dear man.

* * *

Reflections on Love

Nobody tells you when it ends. Well, they shouldn't have to. You can feel it. It's that inner nagging feeling we have that you just need to cry, but because we're grown-ups we suppress it and go on, never really letting the hurt go. In some of us it will brew and manifest itself in bitterness, and that will ensure that you never find love again. Others develop the disease of suspiciousness, always looking to compare the new person in your life with the one who did you wrong. That again will doom you to a life of solitude.

The magic that brings it to us, also takes it away. Why? Perhaps some relationships are only meant for a time. You come together to learn something from each other, and once you have, it's time to move onto the next lesson. But sadly, most of us never learn, and that means a life sentence of bewilderment and confusion and blame.

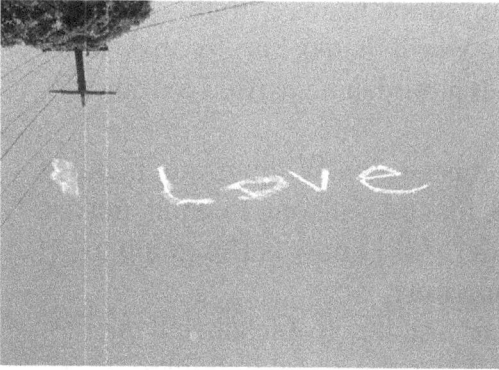

Then we have the serial offenders, those so petrified to be alone they will let anyone in their life, even someone they don't particularly like, and attempt to love them. Those people are not in love with a person, they are in love with a concept.

Rod McKuen once said, "I am not lonely, I'm just alone." And perhaps deep in that is the answer. If you're desperate to love someone, start with yourself. And by that I don't mean become an ego-maniac. When you love someone, really love someone, you love them for who they are, warts and all. Well, to quote that wise Jewish man Jesus, "Physician, heal yourself."

So, today, start accepting yourself for who you really are. With that comes a great inner peace for you're no longer playing a role that you've been miscast in. Even Brando couldn't do that and proved it. Being comfortable with yourself and being honest about who you are, is actually quite attractive to others.

We come into this life alone, and that's how we leave it. It's tough to accept but there you have it. We didn't make the rules. If, along the way, you have found love in someone, or in many, you have been blessed and you need to reflect on that and give thanks, for some never find it at all.

Someone once told me, "When it comes your time to die, if you have at the end of this journey at least two people in that room that loved you so much they'd gladly give their own life so you could live, you've had a wonderful life."

We hang onto things too long. We become collectors. Hoarders. Desperately holding onto things we no longer need, let alone look at. But it somehow gives us comfort to know we own them.

Some people set their own rules for love, as if there weren't enough natural ones too. For instance, age. I, in my time, have lost some wonderful soul mates because I was deemed to be too old or in some cases too young. Yet I don't believe love is based on numbers. You both know it's there, you feel it, until one of you denies its existence. I have loved younger women, I have loved older women. On reflection I wasn't falling in love with the number of years, but rather, with the person. Isn't that how it should be? Or are we too concerned about what our friends will say, or parents, etc., and so we send love away when it comes knocking. And then cry that it didn't come back in a more acceptable package. I think one of the lines I'm proudest of is a song lyric I wrote for "Dear Friend" "... love sees no colour, love knows no age." Yes, it's true, real love is blind.

How do you know when love leaves a relationship? That's easy. You laugh too loud. You talk too much, or don't talk at all. You become exhausted from all the tap dancing to keep the show moving along. We forget that some shows only last one act. Most people don't get a second act in their lives. And rarely a third. Although some us live in hope.

* * *

To Die or Not to Die

Self-destruction. An interesting topic and one that holds a compellingly morbid fascination for most of us. Some of us, especially those who are artists, have dueled with it for years, even choosing the weapons ourselves –

cigarettes, alcohol, and the harder stuff. Are we drawn to these things in order to block out the world or just dull our senses to how hard the road is before us? All the responsibilities that living brings with a new cart load pulling up everyday.

I know a man who is brilliant. Genius even. In a world where the word genius is overused he is the bona fide true meaning. In the same way that the word star got so overused we had to invent the word superstar, this man is a super-genius then, and I love him, warts and all, as a brother. Today he is battling his demons and it's a 50/50 bet on the success of this outcome. But with genius comes the heavy load of having to continually live up to that word in the eyes of others, and to oneself. Oh, what a relief it must seem to just close your eyes and make it all go away. The pressure of outdoing your last triumph or the humiliation of your last misstep hounds you and bites at your heels every step of the way. You are your toughest critic and will beat yourself up more harshly than the best Kenneth Turan could've dished out at his peak. Sometimes, like critics, we are wrong too. Sometimes an orange is just an orange. Or in some cases, a lemon. Do we over complicate our lives by looking too deeply? In the words of Bob Dylan, "Sometimes it's not enough to know the meaning of things. Sometimes we have to know what things don't mean as well."

One day, although my mind has blurred the number of years if not the pain, I was sitting on the stairs of a grand house I once owned, in the depths of despair, having decided to burn the fort and lose everything, my career included, in order to be rid of a business associate neither I or anyone else could trust anymore. My son, Oliver, who must've been only four years of age, saw me and with quite some effort for his little legs climbed the steps up to where I was sitting, sat beside me, put his arm on my shoulder and said, "Don't worry Daddy, it'll be alright when you grow up to be a child." Looking back, I think it's the greatest piece of advice I have ever been told or even read in a book. Therein lies the secret to happiness. Learn to look at life as a child. To appreciate every moment. To take the time to be beguiled by the beauty of simplicity. To look up in wonderment at the falling of a star. Take the time to be silly, it helps you not take yourself too seriously. And to finally realize that if you have a warm bed, and a hot shower, everything else you get is gravy. And be thankful for it.

It is a shocking statistic how many genius artists have died before they lived to 36. Coincidence? Or were they killed by the fear and pressure of having to live up to themselves? When Elvis Presley died his ex-wife showed insensitivity by stating the obvious, "He died at the right time. If he'd lived any longer he would've disappointed us all." Elvis? Now there's an example for you. They say he "officially" died of a heart attack. Cybil Shephard, one of his last girlfriends, has stated that his death is one of the biggest medical cover-ups in history. She said when he died he had enough drugs in his system to still the heart of an elephant, and that, in her opinion, it was the end of a very long suicide. Yes, it's true he never got over losing Priscilla, that's well known, and one can chart his rapid decline from the moment she left him. But was it not more than that? Ironically, the most desired man in the world died of loneliness, surrounded by yes men, a leach of a manager, and women he didn't really love. You see, he'd been too long on Lonely Street. The reality is Elvis died from a lethal overdose of boredom, loneliness, Las Vegas and fear. The fear that it was all past him.

Felton Jarvis, the producer of Elvis' last album "Moody Blue" has said that it was impossible to get Elvis to record the last four songs for that album. In desperation, Jarvis flew to where Elvis was on tour and tracked him down at his hotel, pleading with him to just give a few days of his time to complete the album. ... even just a day! To which Elvis just looked at him and said, "I'm tired of being Elvis Presley." He was dead just weeks later and Jarvis filled out the posthumous album with four live tracks.

And now the great Robin Williams is gone.

But the machine doesn't want to broadcast to everyday folk that people that successful found success that hollow. It messes up the dream that keeps the wheels turning. That dream we all keep chasing and sacrificing to achieve. You mean – I can become king of the world and end up wanting to die? How does that happen? Is the dream just a lie?

I don't know. I'm just a man wandering around in circles in the wilderness like everyone else. But I will share something I have learnt by looking at life from both sides now. Those who think they will be happy once they have money ... or once they have a big car...or once they have a trophy partner ... or once they have a huge mansion ... are in for a jolt. The secret, from one who's learned, is this; you have to be happy before you get those things. Put yourself in order first. And yes, if you are happy within yourself then of course money is the cherry on the cake and will allow you to have some nice times and comfortable living arrangements. Happiness is the foundation on which you build your life. Your inside breeds your outside. Not the other way around. Oh, and when you've got money, help out some true friends. Don't forget that. There is no greater joy than to know you have affected someone's life in a positive way.

In the meantime, send out some positive thoughts to those who are struggling tonight.

* * *

Grains of Sand

If my father had lived
He'd be ninety-three today
And still scratching his head
At life's mysterious play
If I live to be a thousand
And I doubt that today
I would still be blessing
The day he came my way
If my mother had lived
She'd be ninety in July
Still singing this song
Too-Ra-Loo-Ra-Lie

If I live to be a hundred
And I hear what you say
I would still be blessing
The day she came my way
And we're all just grains of sand
On God's eternal beach
Where the wind can blow our
dreams
Just beyond our reach
But I've been honoured to know ya
Both family and foe
Here's a song and a pint
To us all afore we go
T'was your grandmother's dream
To see you turn twenty one
But I'll take her place
And shed her tear, my son
For I'll live to be eighty
If I keep the pipes at bay
And I will still be blessing
The day you came my way
And we're all just grains of sand
On God's eternal beach
Where the wind can blow our
dreams
Way beyond our reach

But it's been me honour to know ya
Both family and foe
Here's a song and a pint
To us all before we go
Never learned a thing at school
Could never follow a rule
They kept losing me
One and one made three
So here I sit
An ignorant git
With a heart as big as the sun
A handshake for everyone
Seduced by the moon
Who dumps me too soon
As the morning catches my sight
I bid farewell to my love, the night
If your daddy don't live
To see ya marry your love
You can bet all your dough
I'll be watchin' from above
When you bow to kiss your
sweetheart
If rain begins to fall
My pride overflowing
It'll be my tears that's all

* * *

A Note to A Son

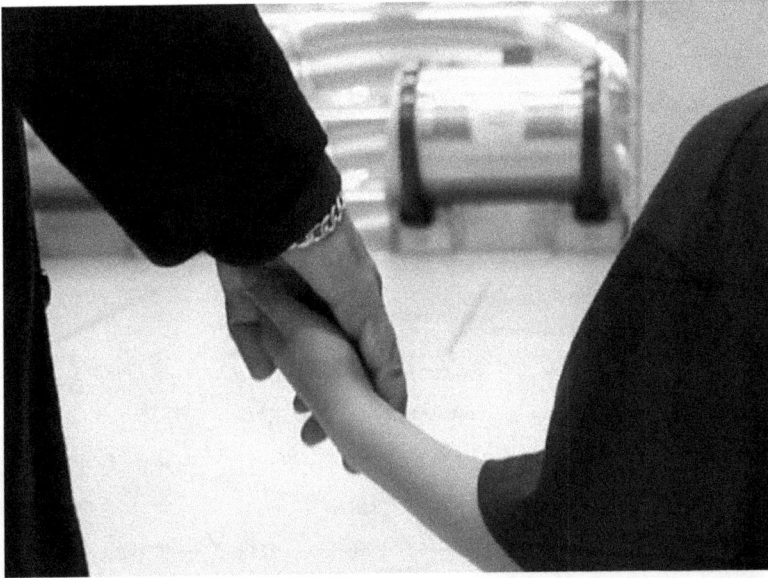

1. Make sure you brush your hair.
2. Smile at old people, it may be the only smile they get all day.
3. Learn everything you can, then forget it and follow your instincts.
4. Play Bob Dylan really loud.
5. Respect the past, but don't live there.

6. Never take no for an answer, even the experts can be wrong.

7. Be kind to children, the one thing everybody deserves is a nice childhood.

8. Watch movies that make you feel something.

9. Believe it or not, your parents were once your age and went through all the same stuff. Sometimes you just need to remind them of that.

10. Make sure you acknowledge the homeless people on the street. There but for the grace of God go us all. And you may be the only person who looks into their eyes all day.

11. The world is a scary place. The world is a friendly place. It awaits your choice.

12. A lot can be achieved with a smile. It's more powerful than a gun as long as it's sincere.

13. At least once a day stop and give thanks for what you have.

14. If you succumb to self-pity, count your friends and you'll realise how fortunate you are.

15. Be bold and mighty forces join you. Nobody ever achieved anything without risk.

16. Make time to occasionally watch the dawn of a new day. It's in that silence that we can hear God's breath.

17. Today is the tomorrow you were worried about yesterday.

18. Hug those you love. It would be a shame if they never realised how much you appreciated them.

19. Make sure you fall in love with a person and not a concept.

20. Don't try and change those you love. Love them for who they are. And ask the same in return.

21. It's true that you have to pass through hell to fully appreciate heaven. 22. Treat every day as a gift. That's why they call it the present.

23. Remember your wise words to your dad once when he was passing though hell, "Don't worry dad, it'll be Alright when you grow up to be a child". I've never forgotten that advice. Don't you ever forget it either.

24. How good a friend you are defines who you are.

25. It's only money. Don't worship false Gods.

26. Love your mother.

27. Try to get a good night's sleep when you can. You'll need it.

28. Whatever happens happens for a reason. Try and learn a lesson from it so you don't have to go through it again.

29. Treat everyone as family until they prove different. 30. Don't trust anything that comes too easy. 31. Create, don't destroy. 32. Don't be cruel.

33. Don't be mean-spirited.

34. Don't be envious.

35. Love this moment. It will not come again.

36. Don't be afraid to occasionally be silly. It's good for you.

37. Learn to laugh at yourself. It saves others doing it.

38. Be humble but never forget who you are. Everyone deserves to be respected. Remind the less courteous if they forget that.

39. Don't allow people filled with darkness into your life. Some will delight in bringing you down.

40. Always tell the truth. A lie is a time bomb that will eventually explode in your face. 41. Be respectful to women. They have it tough enough. 42. At the heart of everything is

the truth. And people will always respond to it. 43. Don't be afraid to ask for help. Or directions.

44. Don't become a slave to anything.

45. Don't surrender your pride, you may never get it back.

46. Stand up for what is right. Even if it's an unpopular thing to do.

47. Don't let someone else's trip become yours.

48. Appreciate every act of kindness done for you. And try and pay it forward.

49. Walk in the park occasionally and observe everything.

50. Angels sometimes bring us messages — make sure you don't dismiss them.

51. Love sees no colour. Love knows no age. You fall in love with someone for who they are, not the colour of their skin or the number of their years.

52. Never make a promise you can't keep. Your word is your bond and a handshake should be the tightest contract in the world.

53. A lot of people will be your friend as long as you're doing what they want. If, the moment it becomes about you, you lose them — they were never your friends to begin with.

54. Never ever forget, for one second, how much you're loved. You were made from love, you are love, now share that love.

* * *

I Remember Grandma

I was going to be named Peter. Well, that's the name my parents had selected for me. That is, until my grandmother arrived at our house to view the new arrival. She was carrying a brand new baby's bath. My parents, who were struggling to make ends meet with two children let alone three, were most appreciative of this expensive gift.

"His name's Frank, y'know!" declared Nana.

"No, it's Peter," stated my equally determined mother.

"I just read a book and the hero in it was Frank, and he was such a lovely person."

But my mother held her ground.

"Anyway, it would make me very happy if you named him Frank after your poor dead brother who's no longer with us." Ah, Nana played her trump card!

But no, I was still to be Peter.

That's when Nana ran into the street, followed by the rest of the family, except me who waited patiently in the front room oblivious of the power struggle I had unintentionally caused. Outside, I was later told, my Nana held the baby bath as high as she could lift it above her head, threatening to throw it into the gutter and smash it into a thousand pieces unless she had her way. That's how I came to be known as Frank. Later, we got a dog. He became Peter.

Probably the earliest memory I still retain is sitting on my Nana's knee in our little kitchen and having her read Noddy books to me. She was a wonderfully spirited, stubborn Irish woman who possessed a wicked sense of humor. Right up until the end of her life she still spoke with a strong accent. She was the only living grandparent I had. For a time.

According to my mother, Nana and I would fight over the children's books and which ones were going to be read. I'd inherited some of her fire.

I wish I could remember more about her than the handful of memories I have. Although one's memory may fade with the years it seems the heart does not. To this day a special bond exists and I still have a framed photograph of her in my room. From all accounts, I was the apple of her eye. A hero named Frank. A lost son returned. I was too young to realize the heavy responsibility that had been placed on my small shoulders.

The last time I saw her alive, we had been on a family outing. When she exited the car in front of her house I cried and refused to let her go. My mother later said it was as if I knew I'd never see her alive again. Nana had to come back to the car three times to try and pacify me. Finally, she said she couldn't come back anymore and, with a smile and a wave, was gone.

I still remember the screaming at our front door that evening. Ken Redman, who boarded at my Nana's house, was hysterical. "It's the old lady! I think she's dead!"

Everyone ran into the street and followed Ken. They forgot about me but I ran too until someone scooped me up into their arms.

I still remember toddling down that dark corridor towards the room full of crying, screaming and moaning.

How could you forget that? I nervously peeked in and saw my Nana on her bed. Uncle Alf was soaping her fingers to get her rings off. No one else knew what to do except scream. The room was filled with grown-ups and regret. Didn't they realize she was only sleeping?

I knew that. I was two years old.

We later found out that she'd arrived home to get her son Bill's dinner but he'd told her he was going out and not to bother. Disappointed at the thought of being on her own that night, she wearily took her hat off and told him to have fun.

It was several hours later Ken came home from the pub and found her.

The doctor said she'd had a beautiful death – whatever that means. The cut on her face had indicated that she'd died before she hit the floor otherwise she'd have put her hands out to break the fall.

* * *

Sydney Carton

The character of Sydney Carton has haunted me most of my life. My first introduction to him was my Mum making me watch the old Hollywood movie version of Charles Dickens' "A Tale of Two Cities" starring one my mother's favorite actors, the beautifully spoken English actor Ronald Coleman. Coleman, as Sydney Carton was, as he was in every role he played, sheer perfection. Dickens' character of Carton is a complex study of the human condition. A man who is brilliant but never achieves the success he deserves or craves because of his humility and his dedication to helping others –

most times to his expense. This trauma of frustration in him manifests itself with excessive drinking and a detached apathy to life around him. A man numbed by disappointment and lack of purpose.

"Sadly, sadly, the sun rose; it rose upon no sadder sight than the man of good abilities and good emotions, incapable of their directed exercise, incapable of his own help and his own happiness, sensible of the blight on him, and resigning himself to let it eat him away."

As a young boy watching an old black and white movie starring mostly dead people, I sat with my Mum in our living room and allowed Ronald Coleman as Sydney Carton to rip my heart out. I remember sobbing at the end of the movie. Heartbroken at how unfair it was that this man should die, and that his death, like his life, would go unnoticed.

Over the years as I grew older, Sydney Carton grew richer in my mind. Through experiences of my own I came to see him differently and with a greater depth to what I, as a young boy, could've understood. Carton is in love with Lucie but can't bring himself to reveal his true feelings to her. When his business partner Stryver tells him of his intention to ask Lucie to marry him, Sydney Carton realizes that unless he makes a move the love of his life will be lost. Carton meets Lucie and reveals his love for her. A love that is so strong and pure that he would lay down his life so that someone she loved would live. But Lucie confesses that she is in love

with Charles Darnay, a wealthy young man who has everything that Carton craves. And now his loved one. Sydney Carton despises him and is jealous of everything he is. When Sydney looks at his reflection in the mirror he states, "A good reason for taking to a man, that he shows you what you have fallen away from, and what you might have been...come on, and have it out in plain words! You hate the fellow."

Throughout the novel several people remark about the similarity in looks between Carton and Darney. They could be brothers. During the French Revolution Darney is arrested as an aristocrat and ordered to stand trial. Carton attends the trial and is appalled at the injustice of the circus in progress before his eyes. Behind Darney in the court stands a mirror and is it impossible for Carton to look at Darney without seeing himself. When Darney is found guilty and sentenced to death by guillotine, Lucie is heartbroken. For most men in Carton's shoes these events would play into his hand and deliver him what he most desires. But few men are Sydney Carton. He realizes it would be no good to win Lucie's love this way because she would forevermore be grieving for the man she truly loved. And what good would such a life be to Sydney Carton? It would be as futile and worthless as the one he was now living. Instead, he hatches a plan and bribes people to help him swap places with Charles Darney on the eve of his execution. He would be making good his promise to Lucie to lay down his life for someone she loved.

When Carton is smuggled into Darney's cell on the night before his execution, and reveals the plan, Darney pleads with Carton..."Carton! Dear Carton...I implore you not to add your death to the bitterness of mine." This is where Darney begins to feel compassion towards Carton. Not only does Darney not want to feel the guilt of Carton's death, but he also cares about Carton's life. The switch is achieved and Darney escapes to join his love, Lucie, while Carton lives out the final hours of what was another man's destiny. But Sydney Carton is now a changed man. Or perhaps the true potential of Sydney Carton has at last been released. He is now calm and filled with a heartbreaking joy that his life will have had some meaning and purpose after all, and that his great love Lucie will have the life he would wish for her.

A young seamstress who awaits the same fate as Carton becomes knowledgeable as to what has happened and is filled with admiration for this man. She confesses how scared she is. Perhaps Dickens modeled her character on Martha, an important woman in the Bible and one of Jesus' followers. When Carton and the seamstress are being herded into carts to take them through the streets of jeering people to their fate, the seamstress says to Carlton, "May I ride with you? Will you let me hold your hand? I am not afraid but I am little and weak, and it will give me more courage."

The seamstress' words are similar to the discussion between Jesus and Martha when Jesus promises the resurrection to the faithful. Jesus said to her, "I am the resurrection and the life; he who believes in Me will never die. Do you believe this?" Martha replied, "Yes Lord."

Through this passage Dickens found a way to demonstrate Martha and Jesus' conversation through the bond between the seamstress and Carton. In the cart on the way to their execution, Carton holds the young woman's hand and as he looks out upon the crowd of jeering angry faces that line the city he loved he has a vision, "I see a beautiful city and a brilliant people rising from this abyss, and, in their struggles to be truly free, in their triumphs and defeats, through long years to come, I see the evil of this time and of the previous time of which this is the natural birth, gradually making exploitation for itself and wearing out."

When Carton and the seamstress reach the guillotine and await their call, Carton tells her to keep looking at his calm face and to think of nothing else. It will be over soon.

And there, as he waited away his last minutes he had a vision of his loved one and her son and hoped that the boy would be told good things about him. "I see that child who lay upon her bosom and who bore my name, a man winning his way up in that path of life which once was mine. I see him winning it so well, that my name is made illustrious there by the light of his. It is a far, far better thing that I do, than I have ever done; it is a far, far better rest I go to than I have ever known."

In "A Tale of Two Cities" Dickens created a character that shows there is a purpose for everyone, no matter how many mistakes were made in the past. Sydney Carton was not a perfect man. But he was a man made perfect by his sense of what was the right thing to do. And then acting upon it. Even though that thing was not as he wished it would be, he rose above his failings and flaws to give his life a purpose it had otherwise been denied.

* * *

Give My Regards To Broadway

I realised at an early age that even the experts and the top CEOs can be wrong. Sometimes the only thing these people who sit behind desks have going for them, is a desk. No one is infallible. And when you start thinking you are, you're believing your own publicity and headed for a fall. We've seen some of the greatest generals and leaders in history eventually stumble on their own ego, and make silly mistakes. For every Napoleon there's a Waterloo. Take it from one who knows.

So, I question things. Bobby Kennedy once said,

"Some men see things as they are and say why. I dream things that never were and say why not."

Although I have worked hard, struggled, persevered, and sweated blood and tears, at times I feel like the luckiest guy in the world. Starting from humble beginnings I went onto co-run Australia's most successful film production company during its heyday. We sold Australian films all over the world at a time you couldn't give them away. Miramax, Paramount, Disney, J&M Entertainment, Skouras, Warners, etc. were just some of our buyers. Unfortunately, a lot of people grew resentful of our success and worked against us. And then, left to our own devices, we became undone by the relentless pressure and massive responsibility to keep topping the last product and raising the bar amidst disappearing money.

All I learned from that is this, there is no formula for success. In fact, every time something or someone succeeds it seems to be for a different reason. Is it destiny? Well, Bob Dylan once said that, before he wrote his first song, he just knew he was going to be the greatest. So I guess one of the ingredients is destiny. What about timing? Certainly. The art of being in the right place at the right time. Would the Beatles have succeeded 10 years before? Or 10 years later? Probably not. They were of their time.

Luck? Yes, of course. But how much of our luck do we make? Sam Goldwyn once said, "The harder I work, the luckier I get." Perhaps luck is really the law of attraction. The Indians have an old wisdom, "The smile you send out returns to you." So perhaps it's true that if we want something bad enough and send out enough positive energy in that direction we are eventually rewarded.

Albert Einstein agreed that "everything is vibrations." We are an energy force and so is the world, so if we get our "vibrations" in synch, the doors to success open.

Art, and especially films and music, is about timing, vibrations and harmony. The Beach Boys once wrote a song about it. So is success about timing? Trust your instincts and don't go against them or get talked into things that don't feel right. The legendary Broadway director and writer Moss Hart once said, "I have succeeded many times and I have failed many times. Every time I succeeded it was for a different reason.

Every time I failed it was for the same reason – I said yes when I meant no." Learn to trust your instincts and to back them.

Discipline? You betcha. You're not going to succeed if you can't get out of bed in the morning. While you're sleeping away your life the other guy is out there working on making his dream come true. Or stealing yours. What you put into something is what you get out of it.

I am blessed that creativity has been my life. It has not only been my love and joy but also my career. Looking back, I could not have wished for anything better.

* * *

Remember?

Remember the days before iPods and iPhones when we actually took the time to talk to each other? Really talk. Remember when you could go out to lunch as an escape from the pressures of work and for an hour could unwind and enjoy a meal without being interrupted by a phone call about something that could obviously wait an hour?

Remember when love was something magical and special and people didn't take each other for granted? Or for a ride. We all rejoiced when there was suddenly free love. Trouble is, like most things, people don't value things that come too easily.

Remember when music was on vinyl and an album was big and had a beautiful cover that actually looked like a work of art and we carried those albums around with us to friends' houses as a badge of pride? They had cover notes. They listed what musicians played on what track. What studio each track was recorded at? Who engineered? What time of day or night had it been recorded? Who had written each song? Who arranged it? Who mixed it? The lyrics. It was important to us to know all these things and to respect those who had participated on our beloved recording. It was difficult to skip tracks so it made you listen to every song and appreciate an album as a whole. Now, music has gotten smaller in so many ways. People download things in inferior sound quality and don't give a damn about who played on it and who else contributed. Now it's all about beats.

Remember when people used to know their neighbours? And actually care about them?

Remember when a dog was a child's best friend and there were so many hills to climb and games to play in the open air? It taught us to use our imaginations. Without a computer screen, we could imagine we were Zorro, Davy Crockett, Robin Hood or Geronimo and play in parks for hours having the time of our life. And were safe.

Remember when the smallest gesture was appreciated and treasured?

Remember when we believed that our vote counted for something? This was in the days before the Whitlam sacking (a Prime Minister elected by the public and dismissed by one man), and Kevin Rudd (another man elected by the public but dismissed by his own party).

Remember when our innocence was lost from three bullets fired in Dallas? A reminder that the world was not a safe place for those who dreamed big dreams.

Remember when your parents took the time to read you bedtime stories?

Remember when an ice cream and a trip to the movies made you feel like the richest kid in town?

Remember when Christmas was spent with all those long gone family members and we laughed as if there would be no tomorrow?

Remember when the days seemed so long that you could easily fit into each one everything you had to do?

Remember the first time you heard the Beatles and they sounded like nothing you'd ever heard before? It's hard for younger people to appreciate their full impact on the way things were. Music, hair, clothing, and attitudes changed overnight.

Remember when you were small and played with children with different coloured skin and didn't even notice?

Remember the excitement of each birthday party shared with your friends?

Remember the smell of your Mum's cooking? It seemed like she was some kind of magician. She always knew what you wanted.

Remember when each day was your friend and another chance for an adventure? Where did we lose that enthusiasm for life? I lost it for a whole decade but have worked hard to regain it. Be thankful for each day no matter what you are going through. Each day is a gift. If you treat it as such it will be.

Remember when radio stations played any and every style of music as long as they thought it was a hit? It was such a weird and exciting mix of Beatles, Frank

Sinatra, Herb Alpert and the Tijuana Brass, Louis Armstrong, The Rolling Stones, Elvis, Anthony Newley, The Shadows, Bob Dylan, The Seekers, Bobby Darin, Paul Mauriat, The Kinks, Tom Jones, Shirley Bassey, Janis Joplin, etc., etc., etc.

Remember when people read books and writers became celebrities?

Remember when Bing Crosby was the voice of Christmas?

Remember romance?

Remember Muhammad Ali in his prime when he glided like a proud eagle in flight?

Remember reading the Old Testament and being scared because God seemed so pissed off all the time? In the New Testament He had, like us all, mellowed by time.

Remember crying over the loss of your first love?

Remember when people took the time to write and post Christmas cards?

Remember Noddy in Toyland?

Remember when the circus came to town?

Remember watching man set foot on the moon and knowing nothing would be the same again? It was scary and exciting all at the same time. In the words of Bob Dylan, "Man has invented his doom, first step was touching the moon ..."

Remember when it wasn't painful to remember?

* * *

Create, Don't Destroy

When I look around at the world today and all its problems, the words of the Indian mystic Sai Baba comes to mind. He once said, "if you take your ego out of the situation, you suddenly see things objectively and solutions to problems become apparent."

Another root to problems is ignorance. The cause of racism is ignorance. Because we don't understand something it gives birth to fear. And fear's brothers-in-law are anger and hate.

I was lucky enough to be a child of the '60s and arguably experienced the greatest decade ever of music. All us children of the '60s believed that a three-minute record could change the world. We certainly saw the power of music contribute to the stopping of an unpopular war.

Never underestimate the power of words to change things. Be it a song, or a movie or a play. Creatives have a big responsibility as to whether to explore the light or the darkness of life. You have the power to influence many, be aware of that and make sure your message is clear and thought out. Hope is a powerful beacon for many who have been shut out of the world. Paul McCartney has said that the thing he's most proud of with the Beatles is that all the songs were about love. Maybe that's why they endure.

Sam Goldwyn, one of the czars of MGM, once reprimanded his writers by saying, "Save your messages for Western Union." So the writers learnt to dress their messages up in entertainment, disguising them in love stories, comedies, horror movies and even musicals. But they are there for anyone with any sensitivity to see.

They dreamed up a better world where there were heroes and where the wronged eventually won in the final reel. It was wish fulfillment on a grand scale and people lined up at the box office to escape the real world and get a glimpse of how things could be in a just place.

So creative talented people – you do have the ability to bring about change. What you create today will influence the future. Change comes about slowly, but it does come. Like the ripple from every stone that's thrown into a lake, each small wave goes on and on.

Writers, directors, producers and actors – It all starts with you. The dreamers, I believe, will always defeat the naysayers. But it does take perseverance, sweat and patience. If you want to do something bad enough you'll always find a way. We sometimes like to put obstacles in our path to give ourselves an excuse for not doing something, or looking the other way, or taking the easy option, but someone once said the only limitations we have are the limitations we place upon our own imagination. The dreamers are looked down upon as the fools in our society but without them we'd still be sitting in a cave wondering how to light a fire.

Go light a fire. We need to shine a light on things to find our way through the darkness.

* * *

The Power of Music

I never took no for an answer. Why? Beats me. Maybe my tough upbringing. Maybe it was ignorance. Sometimes if you don't know what the risks are it makes you incredibly brave. Orson Welles was once asked how, at the age of 25, he could direct his first movie "Citizen Kane" and it go down in history as the greatest film ever made. His answer was, "I was ignorant. I didn't know what the rules were so I broke them all. In fact, I was using John Ford's cameraman, the great Gregg Toland, and one day the legendary old master film director himself John Ford came to the set and asked Gregg how I was doing. Greg replied, "Jack, the kid knows nothing about making a film. He's doing everything wrong and breaking all the rules. And if you tell him what the rules are, I'll kill ya, because he is doing some of the most exciting things I've ever seen."

That's my theory about the Beatles too. They didn't know what the rules were, so they broke them. And music, and the world, would never be the same.

Well, maybe my breaking of the rules wasn't anywhere near the level of the masters I have just mentioned, but the result was the same. Most times when people told me I was mad and that there was no way I'd achieve what I wanted – that's when I had my biggest successes.

Let's face it, if we all followed the formula, then every outcome would be the same. Predictable, safe, boring.

I knew from an early age that I wasn't going to university. So my only other chance in life, it seemed to me, was to think outside the box. Go for the big gamble. Bite the bullet. Roll the dice.

I would be lying if I said every time I followed that advice I won. No sir. Many times I failed and failed magnificently. Losing my money, home and family in some cases. But what is a life if it isn't to be lived? You certainly can't win if you don't place the bet, take the

risk.

Like a lot of kids who weren't great at school I sought refuge in music. At a young age I saw the Beatles on TV and it changed my life forever. They exuded such joy it was contagious. They seemed to be having such fun that you desperately wanted to be in that band with them. I know I did. So I picked up a cheap guitar and started practicing in my room. I dreamed of fame, girls, money and, most of all, experiencing the joy that I saw on the faces of John, Paul, George and Ringo when they played together.

Music and theatre would earn me a living in Australia and take me around the world. But as the great Stevie Wright once sang, "It's a hard road," but for those who go the distance it will bring you a joy that can't be experienced in any other profession. The joy of reaching an audience, touching their spirit and knowing that you've shared a magic moment that may not come again. As I've said, my life has been one of ups and downs but I would not change it for a minute. Even the most despairing periods have taught me valuable life lessons.

Do we choose music or does it choose us? I believe in destiny and a calling. And I think we know, deep down inside, what we've been made for. Sometimes we lose our way. Sometimes the noise of other well meaning people's advice drowns out our own instincts. Sometimes we get scared of taking the leap of faith. But I firmly believe if you were born for it, you will know. And if you know, trust your heart. Your head is full of worries and numbers and doubts. I believe it is through your instinct that the universe, or God, or whatever you want to call it, talks to you. "Be brave and mighty forces will join you."

Life is a long time to live with regret. I may've made mistakes in my life but I have few regrets. Looking back now from the vantage point of maturity I realise that everything that happened to me, both good and bad, happened for a specific reason. A lesson. If you get knocked to the canvas, instead of wasting years whining about it, stop and think about why it happened – and what it has taught you. Once you've learnt the lesson, there will be no need to repeat it.

I remember watching, along with the rest of the world, the great Muhammad Ali make his comeback for the World Heavyweight Championship against Joe Frazier. Ali had been stripped of his championship title by the U.S government because he'd refused to be drafted and go to Vietnam. After sitting out of the ring for several years, years in which he would've been in his prime, the case finally went to court and was dismissed. The judge lifted the ban and Ali was allowed to fight again. Unfortunately, they couldn't give him back his championship title because Joe Frazier now retained it. So, the Fight of the Century was announced and the world waited to see the outcome.

During the fight, Ali, for the first time in his career in the U.S was knocked to the canvas and the whole world gasped. But what moved me, was not that he'd been knocked down, but how quickly he got up. It showed the pride of the man. The great dignity. The courage. The heart.

It is called the music business for a good reason. Music Business. One word does not outweigh the other. Both are equally as important. It's strange the memories that stick with you of your youth. I've always remembered being a young music crazed kid and standing in the middle of the large and impressive Sutton's Music store in the heart of Melbourne city looking around in awe at all the beautiful music instruments proudly displayed. Then gazing at the massive catalogue of sheet music of the latest Top 40 hits of the time. It was one of those defining moments in one's life. I was completely lost in my thoughts imagining how wonderful it would be to work in the music industry. I was suddenly jolted back from my daydream when a salesman asked me if he could help me choose the best musical instrument for me. Sadly, I told him I was just looking, he smiled and told me to let him know if I needed any advice, and then walked away leaving me with my dreams.

I thought how blessed he must feel to work in such a great store, to hear music all day, and to play a part in helping people choose the right guitar or keyboard or trumpet or whatever to set them on their path.

These salesmen become like Gods to me and I hung on every word of advice they gave. Perhaps it was the power of attraction that I set in place that day with these constant dreams. Who knows? All I knew was I wanted to be a part of the music biz and perform and write songs that maybe other people would record.

There is a quote I once read that I love. It's rumoured to have been written by the great Robert Louis Stevenson (author of "Treasure Island", "Doctor Jekyll and Mr. Hyde" etc.). The passage reads "... Down through the ages I have walked with men, yet none have ever fathomed me, with the prince and the beggar I roam the earth and all men love me, for I am the spirit of the very best that is in them, and they praise and strive for the best that is within me. I am the soul of the arts. I am music."

I firmly believe that music, as Mr. Stevenson so eloquently wrote about, is indeed magical and that it lives within our heart and soul, and is indeed the very best of us.

It has been researched in recent years by psychologists that music plays a huge part in influencing our mood. They have sometimes instructed their depressed patients to compile a collection of the happiest songs they can find and to play it while they work out or go for a long walk and report back after a week as to its effect. The majority of people confirmed that their depression was eased and replaced by a much more positive and optimistic outlook. It's ironic that when we go through a relationship break-up we tend to gravitate to listening to songs by Leonard Cohen or other experts in grief and despair and what happens? We get more and more depressed.

Many people listen to various classical music pieces for relaxation and meditation, and swear by its beneficial effects to calm their inner stress. On the other hand, it's not uncommon for factories and business offices to have upbeat background music or "muzak" played to increase productivity.

I don't think it's by chance that for many hundreds of years, just before battle, generals have had soul stirring music played to their soldiers, either on bagpipes, violin, trumpet or drums depending on the culture.

Many people have unfairly blamed Wagner, Hitler's favourite composer, for contributing to the Second World War. Of course that's a laughable exaggeration but it does highlight the potential power of music and how it can be contrived and manipulated for a required effect on the psyche of man.

President Roosevelt personally awarded the Congressional Gold Medal to George M. Cohan for the positive impact his songs had on the morale of U.S. soldiers and citizens alike during wartime. Also, take into account the joyful sounds of the Beatles' early hits.

The Fab Four sent a huge one out into the world and the outpouring of love and joy that came back at them was a staggering phenomenon we may not witness again. It is fitting that the last line of the last song of the last recorded Beatles album is, "And in the end, the love you take is equal to the love you make."

This leads me to believe that the Beatles were smart enough to be well aware of what they were doing. Just as the Rolling Stones' savvy manager Andrew Loog Oldham, realising it was useless for his band to attempt to compete with the Beatles, deliberately went for the opposing market. He contrived his band to be the antithesis of everything the Beatles represented. The Stones purposely dressed to look unkempt and dirty. No Carnaby Street or Saville Row tailored suits for them. They also grew their uncombed hair longer and looked surly in publicity photographs. This proved to be a stroke of genius and they claimed the counter culture. The rebel kids who couldn't identify with the joyfulness of the Beatles music or their lovable image. Of course as time went on and the Vietnam War escalated my idol, Mr. Lennon, steered his boys into more rebellious and revolutionary waters. The icing on the cake was a modern minstrel that called himself Bob Dylan who, as Don McLean described him in his symbol-laden smash hit "American Pie," Dylan dressed in "… a coat he borrowed from James Dean and a voice that came from me and you."

There is no doubt that Dylan sang and played the battle call for a generation of young kids who rejected the authority of their war-mongering leaders and prophetically warned them that the times were indeed a-changing and that they'd "... better start swimming or you'll sink like a stone."

It is well documented that the protest movement undertaken by teenagers in the late '60s was the cause of President Nixon's decision to withdraw U.S. troops from Vietnam. In a war that the U.S still can't believe they didn't win, ironically, they hadn't been beaten by the

Viet Cong but by their own children who had shown the world that they had a voice and it wouldn't be silenced again. Again, just another example of the power of music.

How many people have fallen in love while certain romantic songs have played and these remain "their" song forevermore? If there is a God perhaps it makes perfect sense that He or She invented music and through it is how He/She speaks to our heart.

I can certainly attest to the power of music to change lives. It changed mine. The famous Joseph Campbell who studied the mythologies of all known cultures since the beginning of time and wrote the brilliant book "The Hero With A Thousand Faces" stated, in one of his last TV interviews, that when he was a young man he felt his life was in turmoil and everything that happened to him made no sense. But, looking back at his life from the vantage point of being an old man, he wondered "Who conceived this brilliant scenario?" because it all made perfect sense – "This led to that which led to this" and so on.

* * *

Monogamy & Monopoly

Monogamy and Monopoly – perhaps the same thing really. Bear in mind that every woman smiling at you is potentially a perfumed assassin, but then so are you. Personally, I think having sex with someone you don't care a fig about is like doing push-ups over a warm corpse. On the other hand, should you care, really care, and I have sometimes cared more than it was worth, it's indeed a magical religious-like experience. But know that once you care, you're doomed. Love is a series of small deaths. We fall in love with women because they're sensuous and smart, yet that's the very thing we attempt to close down, reducing them to someone we no longer know, or can relate to, or of interest. Perhaps we're only capable of falling in love with the concept of someone anyway. Some of us go on smashing into the furniture all our lives while others choose to sit in the stands observing the game in play, bemused at the follies of others. Some men kill the thing they love the most. But perhaps I think too much.

* * *

Dear One

She'll be here again tonight and we'll go out and laugh and dine and wine and the world will go away.

She is my dear true friend, who probably knows me better than anyone and just smiles as she reads my mind. She looks at me with love in her eyes and I return that look a thousand fold, as I touch her hand she touches my heart.

She cares, in times of triumph and despair. If I could worship her every night from now to eternity, I would. But the God of such things acts in mysterious ways and perhaps this is love at its truest form. When there are no other agendas or distractions or conditions. She is in my presence and that is enough to be grateful for. Anything else would be an abuse of good fortune.

I have learned to be still. Expectations are for the young and those who never learn. Some things are best left in their pure state. That way they never decay and die. There are no secrets. No demands. No regrets. No competitiveness. We will be friends forever for our souls have touched.

And in the words of Ira Gershwin, "they can't take that away from me." People say we are meant to be together. Little do they know, we are.

* * *

Love

Love, when you think about it, should be the easiest thing. You find someone you love, who loves you, you share, confide, trust, believe in, and respect. And it goes on and on.

But not in this day and age it seems. Well not for most of us. Why is that? Has the world changed so much that love is out of date? Or are we just out of step with it? Do we want too much? Or are we too flighty to settle for anything that smacks of comfort?

How many times have you thought you've found it only to have, after a few years, the bird fly? And why? Do they get scared that it may actually be the real thing and they're unprepared for it? Or do they think something better may exist outside and so off they go only to realize months or years later that it did not and that they have actually killed the very thing they were craving. The very thing that may not come again.
Sex is easy. Any fool can do it.

Love is difficult. It requires trust in a suspicious world. It requires commitment in an undisciplined age. It requires effort from a lazy soul.

Paul McCartney was once asked why, out of all the women in the world that threw themselves at him, he settled for Linda. And he replied that it happened one day when they were walking down the street and she turned to him and said, "Y'know, I could make you a loving home."

To Paul, who had grown with a loving dad and Mum (until her death at too young an age) it had been everything he had secretly craved. Linda had uttered the magic words and she did good on her promise and made his home one filled with family and love until she was tragically taken from him. But they had experienced one of the great loves.

Are we too spoiled to see a great love when it finally appears? Or do we just want to experience it for a night or two before moving on ... to what? The nothingness we have grown comfortable with?

Perhaps we are really only comfortable with ourselves. Perhaps we are so scared of being hurt that we hurt ourselves by denying us the chance of something more.

Or does it run deeper? I remember in the Sixties there was a quote people used to write on walls that said,

"Is God Dead?" Well, perhaps love is dead. I mean, real love.

To give unconditional love means to actually love something more than your own ego. But then, as the Indian mystic Sai Baba once said, "Ego is the cause of all problems in the world. Take your ego out of the way and you see things as they really are. With clarity."

They say you only find love when you're not looking for it. I have to agree. Several times I have found it when I had given up and firmly closed the door. Lost interest. Lost belief. And was content to just watch and be amused by other people's follies. And then it arrives. "Love walks in and takes you for a spin ..."

We live in a cynical age. A fast age. We have the world at our fingertips. We can access any knowledge within seconds yet do we comprehend it? It is impossible to have a conversation in a restaurant anymore without the person you're chatting with accessing their iPhone to check messages, or even returning calls. And maybe that's where the real truth lies. Perhaps we don't have the concentration anymore to develop real relationships. Instead, we settle for convenient ones that don't tax us too much.

Or do we have relationships whilst still keeping an eye on the door lest a better option enter the room? If that is what you're doing, I'd suggest you're not in love. Who knows? And sadly, I'm beginning to wonder, who cares?

* * *

Slandered

Come to think of it, I have been slandered most of my life, one way or another. I guess it's the price you pay for getting off your ass, sticking your neck out, and achieving something. Of course you sometimes stumble, that's comes with the territory and sadly those moments will be the only ones your enemies cling to. It disappoints but makes you harder. At those times it will be difficult to see the humanity in others and to hold onto your belief that at the heart of all things lies a goodness. But in order to do your best work you must struggle to believe in those things even if you are bereft of evidence.

Why do people who know better, or should, slide to slander another? Envy? Ignorance? To elevate themselves at another's expense? Or something far darker?

Wilheim Reich wrote a book entitled "The Murder of Christ" – its conceit was that the murder of Christ keeps on being perpetrated. In a nutshell, all of us are born with a light force but most have it beaten out of us in childhood through dysfunctional parents or a school system that turns circles into squares. Those of us that retain that child-like light force, or positive openness to life, are doomed to ridicule, slander and the spiteful, destructive actions of others. The soul destroying realization is that most of these negative attacks are from those who profess to be friends.

According to Reich these people are mostly unaware of their actions or intentions. It is as if your mere existence irritates them. You see, light will always attract to itself the darkness that cannot rest until it has extinguished it.

The celebrated writer Arthur Miller, who was always reticent to discuss his ex-wife Marilyn Monroe, once said, "It's strange, but that girl seemed to draw to herself the very people who would destroy her."

I have had my integrity attacked by law breakers; my talent questioned by people who couldn't spell their name; my vision ridiculed by hacks who couldn't direct traffic (and then went on to publicly prove it), my sanity tested by the mentally impaired, my compassion thrown back in my face by those whose dictionary does not contain the word "empathy", and judged by thieves in a world where only materialistic items and wealth are valued.

I once stood up over a principal – I refused to work with a man who broke the law. In order to be rid of him I had to burn the fort. And myself. I once told Warren Zevon that story and not long after he wrote a song called, "I Was In The House When The House Burned Down." Yep. I have the scars to prove it.

And yes, the days do grow short when you reach September. My life has been simplified by circumstance and I've paid greatly for that principal. I guess I grew up watching too many Gary Cooper films where the hero risked it all but won in the final reel. But they were just movies. Wish fulfillment. Childish dreams of a more just world.

More people have been murdered by words than by a gun or a sword. There are many killers amongst us who think by spreading unfounded gossip they don't have blood on their hands.

The truth is, in the end, it doesn't much matter to most people. And, sadly, neither does the truth. We live in a modern world where it is no longer respected. People are only interested in the abridged Readers Digest version that they can misquote at dinner parties in-between snorting lines of coke and boring everyone senseless with tales about how busy they are on their journey to death. They get their news from gossip rags like the National Enquirer, or some other celebrity dirt publication. They form their views from Chinese Whispers. They get their music lessons from Nero.

Your only reward in a Spartan life is to sleep the sleep of the just. And being able to look at your own reflection without flinching.

* * *

For Nicky

He always wanted to write
"The Night They Drove Old Dixie Down"
Although he didn't understand it
He wanted to incorporate it into one of his poems
It took him back to a time

And the great love
Both now gone
Even he, now, is gone
He had so many friends
He had none
I miss his chuckle
His observations
His view of a world gone mad
He was cool
Needed jazz as an underscore
Had a heart as big as the twinkle in his eye
That refused to die

Like an old soldier
He only knew war
And secrets
And betrayal
I wish he'd stayed around long enough
To see that it was sunny
And that his words
Could have been his escape

I miss ya, Nicky

* * *

Booze & Drugs

There's a great scene in "Breaking Bad" where Walt White and Hank, his DEA brother-in-law, discuss the thin line between what's legal and what's not. And that even good people can topple over sometimes onto the wrong side of the line for the simplest of things.

Much has been made of Robin Williams' on and off drug problems and struggle with alcohol, but I would suggest when he decided to end it all he was straight.

On October 28, 1919 – a date that will live in infamy if not the annals of stupidity – the U.S. Congress passed the Volstead Act over President Wilson's veto and prohibited the sale of alcohol to the public.

And what was the effect of that? It made gangsters like Al Capone very wealthy men. By 1925, in New York alone, there were, estimated, between 30,000 and 100,000 speakeasy clubs. The moral of the story? If people want something bad enough they'll get it. Making it illegal just insures that you have to pay inflated prices for it and deal with criminals and underworld characters that brings with it its own dangers.

When Hollywood previewed the Brian DePalma remake of "The Untouchables" they found they had a major problem with it. The audience were rooting for Al Capone over the do-good law enforcement Prohibition Agent Eliot Ness. And why not? The latter was hell-bent on denying the public booze. So the studio had to shoot an extra scene early in the movie that showed Capone's men placing a bomb in a store that wouldn't pay protection money and a little kid was killed, thus turning the audience's sympathy from Capone to Eliot Ness.

So, in those dim dark ages, if you knocked three times on a speakeasy door and gave the right password, you were let in to have a scotch or a gin or whatever alcoholic beverage you were seeking. Oh, and you were considered a criminal.

Alcohol was banned to stop people over-indulging. That's like banning food because some people over-eat. I think it's always a very dark and sinister act when the government attempts to control what should be, in a free society, one's personal choice and responsibility.

I would argue that cigarettes have killed more people than alcohol. Why don't we ban those? And how ineffective would that be? Again, we'd just give a lot of criminals a new business opportunity and make them a fortune. And we'd end up paying $100 for a pack of cigarettes.

In 1922, during the alcohol prohibition years, cocaine was also banned and thus another substance, that had been legal and freely available, was given over to the underworld to boost their pockets.

The celebrated Austrian psychoanalyst Sigmund Freud, himself a cocaine user, prescribed the substance to his patients believing it was a cure for depression and sexual impotence. In 1884 he published an article "Uber

Coca" which promoted the "benefits" of cocaine, calling it a "magical" substance.

In 1886 it got a further boost when John Pemberton included coca leaves as an ingredient in his new soft drink, Coca-Cola. This new drink was also considered to be, ironically, a cure for a hangover caused by an over-indulgence in alcohol.

During the early 1900s, cocaine and opium-laced elixirs (magical or medicinal potions), tonics and wines were broadly used by people of all social standings. Notable figures who promoted the "miraculous" effects of cocaine included inventor Thomas Edison and actress Sarah Bernhardt.

By 1905 it became popular to snort it. By 1912 The United States government reported 5,000 related deaths in one year due to an over-use of cocaine. By 1922 it was officially banned, which, when news reached Sherlock Holmes it probably resulted in his suicide by throwing himself off the Reichenbach Falls.

So, like alcohol, it was not the substance itself that was lethal but rather some people's over-use of it. Did you know if you drink too much water you can die from it? All we need is 5,000 of us to do that in any one year and perhaps they'll ban that too.

What I'm getting at is where does one's own personal responsibility come into it? And where's the line where the government intervenes into our lives and criminalizes something because some people are over-indulging?

I used to listen to a talkback radio guy in L.A who was a Libertarian. Their political philosophy upholds liberty as the principal objective. Libertarians seek to maximize autonomy and freedom of choice, emphasizing political freedom, voluntary association and the primacy of human judgment.

A woman's debate about the right to abortion is that "it is my body and the government does not own it and anything I wish to do with it should be my choice and not theirs."

Well then, it you want to take that debate further, and not that much further, isn't it also correct that if I own my own body then I should be allowed to do whatever I want with it? Is it not my own personal choice if I want to drink a gallon of scotch, or shoot up heroin, or snort cocaine, smoke a carton of cigarettes, or my smelly socks for that matter? And if I've had enough of this life isn't it also my right to end it? Surely it only becomes a matter for law enforcement if we are intoxicated, or high or suicidal and get behind the wheel of a car? Because by doing that we are putting other people's lives at stake. People who have chosen to want to live. Then, of course, it is a concern for society at large.

John Lennon once had a hit with a song that said, "Whatever gets you through the night is alright ..."

I try to get through this life attempting to be as non-judgmental of others as possible. Unless of course they steal from me or attempt to harm me. If someone is struggling and needs prescription drugs to get through, or need to self-medicate themselves with something that makes them feel better, what business is it of ours? My sympathy is with them that need it, and also my prayers. But to judge Robin Williams or Jim Morrison or Heath Ledger or Elvis or any of the millions of people out there is an act of arrogance and shows a severe lack of empathy for the pain they may be carrying. Perhaps those people who sit in judgment in their ivory towers need to come down and fuck themselves.

How do you end the drug wars and get rid of the criminal element in one swift and effective move? You legalize it. At least then there would be some monitor on exactly what people are taking and what amount. And perhaps if it is noticed that some are in such pain they are over- indulging then maybe some counseling could be recommended. But again, it would be one's personal choice as to whether they accepted that or not.

In California now and in some other U.S. states "pot" is legal with a medical prescription. Have people gone mad with it? Of course not. They buy what they need to get them through the week and go home. Like buying a six-pack of beer.

Believe it or not Richard Nixon was the first President that believed drug addicts should not be treated as criminals but instead needed counseling. It would certainly free up law enforcement officers to focus on more important crimes, like people murdering each other. Or the next terrorist attack.

And besides, I would've thought the Government would prefer us all to be medicated anyway, so that our anger would be numbed to what idiots they are.

Anyway, just thinkin' out loud.

* * *

Fawkner Street, St. Kilda

Nowadays St. Kilda is a highly sought after area and has attracted the trendy market of home- buyers. In the Fifties and Sixties it was a whole different story. Growing up in St. Kilda taught you to be tough, alert and street wise. Sometimes your life depended on it.

Fawkner Street St. Kilda was a notorious and sometimes dangerous shortcut to Luna Park. It was a street I was brought home to as a baby in my proud mother's arms. At that time it was also home to some dangerous criminals such as the Shannons, Norm Bradshaw and Pretty Dulcie.

Growing up in that street gave you a few interesting options in life, you could either learn to be a gangster yourself, or else, if you were of a more sensitive nature, you could observe the human condition in all its most glorious and contradictory terms. As a budding actor or writer you were truly blessed by the abundance of original characters that performed every day in the street theatre outside your window. They could ignite the curious spark in the fertile creative brain of a lonely child.

Norm Bradshaw was associated with Freddie "The Frog" Harrison and they were eventually charged with the attempted murder of a gangland rival, George Newman. Normie and Freddie attached a Tommy Gun mounted on an open window of a taxi. They drove past Newman's Vauxhall Sedan and sprayed it with bullets. Nifty Newman survived but the court case fell over when a key witness failed to attend to give evidence. He later re-emerged to tell police that his failure to do so was a result of being informed his house would be bombed if he showed up. Bradshaw and Harrison were found not guilty by a nervous jury.

Normie was known as "The Beast" – and for good reason. One night he threw lighter fluid over his girlfriend and set fire to her. And that was someone he loved! She obviously loved him too and remained with him after the incident. Why? It's hard to fathom. But it highlights something about the walking contradiction of these dangerous and hard men – they could either be your worst nightmare or disarmingly charming depending on what the situation required. Sometimes zig-zagging between both within hours, minutes – even seconds.

As a small child I remember my parents holding a fundraiser in our small modest living room for my eldest sister who was an entrant in a beauty pageant. The evening was teetering with the group of friends and acquaintances who'd come to party and donate to the young girl's dream of becoming Miss Victoria. Halfway through the festivities a knock came to the front door. My Mum answered it only to find Norm Bradshaw standing there with one of his henchmen.

"I don't want any trouble, Normie!" said my fearless Mum.

Normie smiled and answered, "No trouble, Mrs. Howson. I'm here to help the little girl. How's the fund-raising going?"

My Mum stated the truth, "Slowly." To which Normie relied, "Well, we'll see about that. Give me the hat."

He then went around to everyone at the party, gave them the killer stare and asked how much they were contributing to the cause. Of course everyone emptied their pockets making the evening a roaring success.

So many times, with these characters, kindness walked hand in hand with brutality. Normie was known to many as a killer, a stand-over man, a psychopath, and other unsavoury things. But in our little home that night, he'd been Robin Hood.

Some months later, my Dad and Mum were awakened from their sleep by raised voices in the street outside our window.

Dad got up and peeked through the venetian blinds. Outside, Norm Bradshaw and an associate were involved in a verbal argument with a third man. This resulted in Normie bringing the debate to an abrupt end by punching the agitator to the ground. He and his henchman then began to walk away but were stopped in their tracks by something the fallen man said. Normie, slowly, turned around, walked a few paces closer to the third man, produced a revolver from his inside coat pocket, and shot the man dead. He then continued back home with his friend.

My Dad, being a quick thinker, instructed my Mum to help him move the bed to the back of the house. He then moved the living room furniture up to the front room. When the police knocked on our door and questioned my father as to whether he'd seen or heard anything during the night, he replied in the negative, stating that, as the bedroom was at the back of the house, he hadn't heard a thing. The police checked this out for themselves and then went on their way.

A short time later there was another knock at the door. This time it was Norm Bradshaw. "Hello Jacky" beamed Norm, although his eyes were as cold as ice.

"Good morning, Norm," replied Dad.

"Just wondering how you've been sleeping lately, Jacky?"

To which my Dad answered, "Like a baby, Norm."

Norm gave another smile – this smile was far more relaxed, "That's all I wanted to know, Jacky. Have a good day." And off he went.

My Mum and Dad continued to sleep at the back of the house for some time.

Most of these criminals were involved in sly grog shops and illegal gambling dens, and as such many disputes resulted from rivals wanting to move in on the action for a cut of the fast money.

Pretty Dulcie was known as "The Angel of Death." She ran a sly grog trade out of her St. Kilda home and had also been charged with soliciting on many occasions. She was our next-door neighbour. One night a wild party she was hosting was interrupted by some uninvited gangsters kicking in her front door and walking down the passage way unloading their guns at the moving targets of party-guests. Dulcie was shot in the hip and her boyfriend Gavin Walsh was killed. Several stray bullets ended up going through the wall into the Howson residence, where we were having a nice dinner in front of our radiogram. If the bullet had've been a little lower and to the right you would not be reading this now.

Another resident of Fawkner Street, St. Kilda was the notorious abortionist Dr. Bertram Wainer. In 1967 a woman had come to Dr. Wainer's surgery seeking emergency treatment after a backyard abortion gone wrong. Dr. Wainer helped the woman and thus began a quest by him to have the abortion laws abolished. At the time abortion was punishable by an up-to fifteen-year jail sentence. Wainer placed an ad in the Sun News Pictorial, under the heading "Abortion Abortion Abortion" and called on women to "not be intimidated by bullying tactics (of the police)." Wainer went on to flag police corruption in protecting the backyard abortionists. After that he became a marked man but went down in history as a crusader for the acceptance of abortion.

No doubt the experience of living in this area had a profound influence on me. As did my father's stories about courage, gladiators, cowboys and warriors. He instilled in me the importance of doing the right thing, no matter what the cost. Sometimes I wish I hadn't learned the lesson as well as I did. It has cost me a lot of money over the years but I sleep well.

I was also blessed by the influence of another great human being, my Mum. A beautiful soul who, if she hadn't been my mother, would still have been my best friend. Without her positive influence in my corner perhaps I too would've run off the rails. In St. Kilda it was an all too easy option to get caught up with the wrong crowd.

The early to mid-Seventies was the "Glam" rock era in music and brought to fame such androgynous performers such as David Bowie, Marc Bolan, Lou Reed, Gary Glitter, Roxy Music, Elton John and saw the rise, probably as a backlash to the times, of skinhead gangs in Melbourne. They were not quite the "national front" type of skinheads, the far right racist extremists that were later to emerge in Britain and Australia. In fact, I don't think our local skinheads and sharpies had any particular ideology, but they liked to think of themselves as "tough." They wore their hair closely shaved with rat tails at the back, and drop cross earrings. (In the left ear – the right one signaled you were gay and that brought its own problems), tight striped cardigans, flair trousers and platform soled shoes called "hoppers."

Being a Beatles tragic I was definitely a devoted and loyal Mod. This meant of course that I sometimes took my life in my hands just going to the movies. But another valuable lesson learned from my Dad was about pack mentality, which would prove useful in life. Always take on the big guy first. If he falls all his underlings soon lose their false bravado. Oh, and it helps if they think you're a bit crazy. Even the most hardened criminal will avoid dealing with a mad man. They are too unpredictable. Chopper Read later confessed to me that he'd spent a good deal of his life establishing that persona as his protection shield.

In the early Sixties I got my first job, in that now extinct profession – selling newspapers on street corners. My designated location was on Fitzroy Street. A very rough and tough place in those days. It taught me responsibility, the pride in working hard to earn money, and how to deal with the public. You meet 'em all – the kind people and the arseholes. It was good grounding in understanding the psychology of the public. What I soon discovered was that even the most cynical, horrible, difficult person, at the heart of it, just wanted to be loved and treated with some respect. Instead of antagonising them, I would continue to smile, send out a positive vibe, and usually that was enough to turn a lot of these people around. Sometimes someone who'd initially been arrogant or mean, would melt into a nice person once their guard slipped. Some of them became my best customers. Arrogance is usually a cover for low self-esteem and high insecurity. Another lesson – politeness and respect go a long way.

My father worked a second job most nights at a sideshow alley near Luna Park. Again, this was invaluable experience for me observing how my Dad and other spruikers dealt with the public. I was learning the art of selling ..." step right up, step right up, folks!"

And to this day, the show goes on.

* * *

A Babe Ruth Story

One day, Oliver Howson was playing baseball on the lawn outside his Dad's apartment.
His Dad had just gone upstairs to get a cool drink for the both of them, and Oliver was practicing throwing his baseball up in the air and catching it in his new mitt. Suddenly, he heard a voice. A loud gruff old voice which made him immediately look up. Well, he couldn't believe what he saw. There, in front of him, framed by the glaring sun, was a big man in a baseball outfit.

"That's pretty good, Oliver," said the man. "Y'know, when I was your age I practiced catching the ball all the time. The more I practiced, the better I got."

"Yeah, that's what my Dad says," replied Oliver.

"Well, he sounds like a pretty wise sorta guy," smiled the big man.

"He sure is," said Oliver, "He's my Dad!"

"Y'know somethin', boy?"

Oliver nodded his head.

"I used to play baseball for a livin'."

Really?" answered Oliver.

"Yep. I played for the Boston Red Sox for a time. Then the New York Yankees. Then the Boston Braves. Didn't do too bad either. Long time ago, that is. Way before you were born."

"Wow, that is a long time ago," said the boy. "I started out practicing in my small back yard. As I said, I worked on catching the ball in my mitt. Then I worked on throwing it fast and mean. I practiced and practiced and practiced until I could throw the ball so fast the batter'd be out before he'd even seen it go past!" Oliver laughed.

Then I worked on batting, and I became so good at it I hit 714 home runs!" Oliver was mighty impressed. "Wow, that's a lot!"

"Sure is, boy. But you know somethin'? It was fun. I found somethin' I liked doing and I practiced and practiced until I was really good at it. Y'know, I wasn't a very fast runner. And I wasn't a great basketball player. Or, a football player. But, baseball, I loved it the first time I picked up a ball and a bat. That's the secret to bein' good at somethin', boy. Fall in love with it. Then while you're having fun, and playing it over and over, you get better and better! It worked for me anyway."

"Thanks, I'll take your advice ... Mr ...?

"Ruth. George Ruth. But people call me Babe." And with that, the man held out his big hand and shook Oliver's.

"Would you like me to sign your bat?"

"I sure would, Mr. Ruth." With that Oliver excitedly fetched it and the big man signed some words on it. Then the Babe looked up at something in the distance and smiled.

"Looks like your father's back with those drinks for ya."

Oliver turned his head and saw his Dad coming towards him carrying a couple of glasses of ice cold lemonade.

"Yeah. That's my Dad alright," said Oliver. He then turned to smile at Babe Ruth, but he was gone.

"Sorry it took me so long, son," said Dad.

"Hope you haven't been lonely."

"Nah Dad. Guess what?!"

"What?"

"I was practicing catching, when Babe Ruth came over to give me some advice."

"Babe Ruth?"

"Yeah, Dad. He was just here! But I thought he was dead."

Dad looked at Oliver and smiled. But it was a sad kind of smile.

"What's the matter, Dad?"

"No, son. People like Babe Ruth never die. They live on in the hearts and hopes of people. Well, I just wished I'd have gotten the chance to meet him. Do you realise how lucky you are?"

Oliver knew.

"What did he say, son?"

"All the things you told me, Dad. Every word. Exactly. All about practicing. And working at what you love doing. He's pretty smart!"

This time Dad gave a really big smile. Followed by a really big hug.

"You know, son, when I was a boy. Just about your age. My Dad told me a story about Babe Ruth. It was about Babe when he was getting old and it looked like he wouldn't be playing baseball much longer. And one day, he was sitting on the bench waiting to go out

247

onto the field and bat, when one of his team-mates noticed how tired Babe looked. Really tired. The team-mate said, "Babe, why don't you go home? We're going to win this game easy, so you may as well take the day off and get some rest. You're not as young as you used to be, y'know?"

But Babe just looked at his team-mate, and smiled. "Thanks, Buddy," he said. "But I ain't going nowhere but out there. And when I get out there I'm going to be trying as hard as I was in my first game to hit a home run!"

"But why?" said his team-mate. "You're the great Babe Ruth! You've got nothin' to prove to anybody anymore. You're in all the history books they'll ever write about baseball!"

"That's not the point," said the Babe. Then his eyes looked out at the distant faces of all the thousands upon thousands of excited people that filled the giant stadium that afternoon.

"Somewhere in that crowd," continued Babe, "A young boy has come today to see Babe Ruth hit a home-run. And it may be the first and the last time he ever gets to see me. And I'm gonna be doin' and givin' everything I can not to disappoint him!"

And that day, Babe Ruth walked out to the plate real slow. He held his bat up into position, looked at the ball in the pitcher's hand, said a silent prayer, and gave it everything he had. And you know what? He hit a home-run right out of the stadium and a lot of boys went home happy. So did Babe."

"Oh, I forgot. Babe Ruth signed my bat! Tell me what it says, Dad."

His father looked at the bat and tears welled in his eyes.

"What is it?"

"It's a message for us all, son. It says "Don't let the fear of striking out get in your way.""

Then Dad and Oliver played some baseball. And when Dad threw the ball Oliver hit it as hard as he could and the ball flew right over Dad's head and into the neighbour's backyard. That day Oliver Howson felt what it was like to be Babe Ruth.

(written for my son long ago when we were separated by distance, not love.)

* * *

Soldier of Fortune

I was in Germany. A little town in the Celle district called Winsen Aller. I had been sent there to executive produce a comeback album of sorts for John Paul Young, which resulted in the Top 10 hit "Soldier of Fortune." This was in the early '80s and I was still young, and not that well travelled, so it was a huge thrill and adventure for me.

I had signed JPY to a contract with the Australian arm of IC Records which, at that time, was the major independent label in Germany. The label was owned by the legendary Klaus Schulze, (ex-Tangerine Dream & electronic music visionary).

I got to hang out with Klaus and once foolishly tried to drink with him. It was a long lunch, well what I remember of it. We drank a bottle of scotch each. The difference was, he was still having a coherent conversation, and I was speaking in tongues. He won whatever macho drinking game was being played and I crawled back to my apartment to die. If I could've phoned room service for an assassin, I would've.

But I loved Klaus, he was charming, smart and a joyous soul to be around. He loved life and in return it loved him back. Not that he was short on love. He was then married to Renata, one of the most beautiful women I had seen, and it was hard to look at Klaus when you were together with them. She was an eye magnet. A movie star without a movie. A model without a runway. She simply ... was. She took the breath out of every room she walked into. Ah, but I digress.

It was the '80s and it was good to be young and in the music business.

I remember that it took something like 27 hours to reach Germany from Australia by plane in those days, given all the stopovers. Having boarded a night flight from Melbourne, by the time I arrived in Hamburg I'd been awake for several days. I was met at the airport by one of the German record company execs who escorted me to his car and drove me to various friendly stopovers of his pals and business associates, who thought what I needed was whiskey, marching powder and slaps on the back. By the time I reached our hotel I was ready to fight the heavyweight champion. My escort

and host suggested that I take a quick shower, jump into a change of clothes and join him downstairs for a drive to the red-light and disco district of Hamburg – the place made famous by the Beatles years before when they were honing their craft. What any sensible man would've said was, "Thank you so much for your kind offer, but I think I'll have an early night and see you in the morning." Instead, fuckwit on parade replied, "Give me 30 minutes and I'll see you in the foyer." I must confess that good sense has abandoned me on occasion.

I forget how many clubs we went to, how many girls we chatted to, and how much outrageously expensive champagne was consumed, as things sped by in a multi-coloured blur.

When I asked Mein Host why the crappy champagne was so expensive he told me it included sex. I quickly peered into the empty bottle but was unmoved. I suddenly feared it may be some kinky German sex game involving shoving the bottle where the sun don't shine. I looked at him suspiciously and sat rigid determined not to give him an opening. "No, silly boy," he said. "Once you buy the girl the bottle of champagne she is yours to do whatever you like!" As it was now very late in the night and I had lost all feeling in my legs, I was a little peeved that it'd taken so long for my new pal to divulge this important detail. In fact, I'd been rather worried that he had a bladder problem as he'd made various trips out back and spent, I'd assumed, a half an hour in the toilet each time. Now it all made sense. He was visiting the champagne girls. No doubt taking my turn as well. If my hands hadn't been numb I may have hit him.

Y'know when you've been awake so long you finally get a second wind and feel like superman? No? You lucky bastard. Suddenly I was energized, speeding off my face, drunk and looking for a future wife. People on the street must've recognized the look as they side-stepped out of my way. I was a man on a mission. Not quite sure I remembered my name or the reason I was in town, but hey, here I was!

"Fancy some more shit champagne, my dear old friend and buddy?" I stammered. Yep, my new pal was up for anything. In fact, I don't think he'd have needed much encouragement to storm Poland.

The next day was slightly more disciplined. Slightly. I was relocated to the large building that housed the IC Records operations in Winsen Aller and shown to my lovely room in the guest wing. I remember my dear Mein Host that perhaps he should speak to Klaus and throw a party for me that night. Invite all the record company people and their publishers, business associates, etc. I must admit to a young man with diminished brain cells it sounded like a jolly good idea.

He drove me into the city and introduced me to their music publisher. I don't remember a thing about him other than his secretary was even better looking than Renata. It is my shame that I've forgotten this girl's name but I was suffering brain damage at the time. What has never diminished is how radiant she was. To this day I can still see her in my mind's eye. Gorgeous beyond belief. I wanted to sign a hundred-year contract with her immediately. When we were leaving I suggested to Mein Host that we should invite the very lovely secretary to our party. Agreeing it was a good idea he did just that, in German. I prompted him to tell her how much I liked her, and he waxed lyrical with more guttural sounds of the German language. She smiled and giggled and flashed those dark eyes at me. God knows what he said, but she accepted. She explained that she'd have to be picked up and taken home after the party. She was indeed a lady, thought this romantic fool. Mein Host replied in the affirmative and the date was set. I was in heaven. But I was young. I was an idiot. And I had not learnt the lesson that there is no loyalty among men when there is such a prize at stake.

The location for the party was at a recording studio in Hanover. I couldn't wait to see the girl. There was only one girl now. I couldn't wait to see her. The hours until the party dragged by and finally I was there. Mein Host then split to pick up the girl and I absent-mindedly chatted and attempted to make small talk with the other guests.

An hour must've gone by. Where were they? Perhaps there'd been an accident. Surely not? Life couldn't be that cruel could it?

I watched the clock in between sips of wine and nodded at people chatting to me in German. Then heads turned to look at the door. So did mine. And she was here.

She smiled at me and made her way over. She didn't walk, she glided as her hips sashayed Monroe-style. She obviously knew the reaction this had on foolish men and I didn't want to disappoint her by seeming aloof. Was it too early in the night to propose? Trouble was, I couldn't understand her and she couldn't understand me. But we spoke with our eyes and it was good. It just felt ... good. After several hours of playing charades I was exhausted and went to refill our glasses. When I returned she was gone. So was Mein Host. I was frantic. Surely they hadn't disappeared on me? I asked those who remained where they'd gone and someone summoned up enough words of English to explain that Mein Host had driven the girl home. I explained that they must be mistaken as Mein Host had to also drive me back to Winsen Aller so there's no way he could leave without me. Surely? "Oh no, didn't he tell you? You're sleeping upstairs tonight at this studio. There is a beautiful apartment on the first floor. All the top recording stars have stayed there." At this point, I wanted to kill my dear departed friend.

I was the one who'd talked him into inviting the girl in the first place. He had seen this girl many times before at the publisher's office and no doubt would see her many times in the future. So why the rush to sweep her away tonight? I guess the old competitive streak had risen in him and a game was being played out.

I spent a sleepless night in the apartment all the top recording stars had stayed in and hoped that the phone would ring and it'd be the girl. But no one phoned. I just hoped she was alright. I honestly cared about her. In fact, I'd been busy all night planning our life together.

At about 10 a.m. after my tenth cup of black coffee, Mein Host sheepishly appeared. He looked hung-over and as exhausted as me. No, actually, more exhausted than me.

I tried to remain calm. After all, I was a guest in a foreign country, and a diplomat for mine.

"You certainly left abruptly?" I stated.

"Yes ... ah ... she wanted to leave."

"Really," I growled, not convinced. "So you drove her home to her place, huh?" " Ah ... no ... We ... she ... well I thought it might be easier if she stayed over at Winsen Aller."

"Oh?" I pressed on. "At your place?"

"Yes. She actually slept in your bed."

I gripped the coffee cup with so much disappointment it's a miracle it didn't snap.

He then broke down and confessed all the details of the night. According to his version she almost raped him. Part of me, desperately seeking any sign of something positive, hoped it was because of the verbal foreplay she'd enjoyed with me. Surely I could salvage something hopeful from this nightmare story unfolding before me?

Mein Host said as soon as he led her into my room she become amorous.

Perhaps the scent of my things had sent her wild? I was clinging to any passing delusion at this point. He went on to say she was quite mad. Okay, well that's never put me off a woman before. Go on. He then said she'd asked for candles and when he brought them to her she lighted them, then slowly unbuttoned her dress and let it fall to the floor around her ankles. She stood there in the candlelight, proudly naked before him. I wasn't sure I wanted to hear anymore. Perhaps I was crying. Or, to quote James Taylor, "in my mind I'd gone to Carolina." But, nothing could shut him up now. As I scanned the room for a heavy object to hit him with, he went on to state for the record that what he saw was a vision of perfection that he would never ever forget until his dying day. Little did he know his demise could be quite imminent.

Fuck, I thought, who do I have to sleep with to stop this story? I was even prepared to play the kinky German bottle game if it'd shut him up.

But no, on and on he went.

She told him she couldn't make love unless he married her. So they performed their own wedding ceremony there in my room, surrounded by the candles. Then she stripped him, tied his hands and ankles to the bed, my bed, dripped the hot wax all over his body and spent the night ravaging him. She was insatiable. Yep, that was the final dagger to my heart. The thought that it may be over between me and my new bride-to-be was chiseling its way into my brain. A few negative electrical shocks ripped through my body. And I felt a burning sensation in my lap before realizing I had spilled the coffee. Or perhaps it just leaked out of my open mouth. Being a polite person I waited until he had finished the story before I killed him. The judge, hearing the tale, found me guilty but gave me a suspended sentence. A lifetime of being suspended in space remembering the girl.

* * *

The Spicks and Specks of My Life

"Give my regards to Broadway, remember me to Herald Square ..."

That was the first song I ever sang publicly, back in the day before the Titanic sailed on that fateful maiden voyage. Or so it seemed. I performed it at the St. Kilda Town Hall and my Mum said I was "brilliant!" Not sure the rest of the audience agreed but who cared? If your Mum was in your corner, life was pretty good.

There was a large age difference between myself and my elder sisters. I'd been a change of life baby and a big surprise to everyone. My parents were overjoyed to have a baby boy in the family and my sisters never forgave me. I guess they thought I'd upstaged them or something. I tried to explain on many occasions that being born wasn't my fault but no negotiation was ever entered into. As a result of all this – the more my mother praised my accomplishments, the more ridicule, criticism and scorn was heaped on me by my sisters. I guess it grounded me. Even to this day, any accomplishment is tainted with an inner voice decrying it as a fraud. Or a fluke.

My father was the loveliest man in the world – up to ten drinks. After that he'd walk the house looking for something or someone to blame. At these times it was best to choose your words carefully. Even a young kid learnt that.

If we got through an evening without my father erupting it was indeed an achievement. On many nights I was a witness to World War III taking place in our living room. Dying room was probably a more apt description. I in fact saw many things die in that room. Love, respect, pride, compassion, dignity, innocence and other casualties of battle now lie in unmarked graves.

There was nothing my father wouldn't say to win a war. His words were bullets that tore your heart out. He had the knack to sense your deepest vulnerability and could, with a few well- chosen sentences, devastate your ego forevermore. No child should've seen or heard what went on in that house, but I was born into this. You either learn to go on, or go nuts. And never, but never, show that you've been hurt.

Most nights I would try to referee the fights but it was no use. It was as though I couldn't be heard. So I would just retreat into my room and turn up the music.

Some years ago I realized that I have continued to do this most of my life.

My father never told me he loved me. You had to learn to read that in his eyes. He had lost his own mother when he was two, and had been denied maternal love. His father drank and gave his kids up to relatives to be brought up. As soon as my dad and his brothers were old enough they'd gotten jobs as stable boys. I remember him telling me it'd been a hard life and that some of the trainers used to get drunk and beat them for entertainment.

When I was living in Los Angeles in 2001 my then wife, Terri Garber, asked why I spoke so lovingly about my father. She said, "From what you've told me about him he was a monster." Monster? No, he was my father. Never underestimate the loyalty of children. Even the child that still lurks within a grown man.

Someone not long ago said to me, "Y'know, when you laugh or get excited about something there is a little boy quality in your eyes. Something innocent and joyous." Perhaps it's the little boy from Fawkner Street, St. Kilda. He ran away from home – or went to his room to turn up the music – or just went and hid somewhere deep inside and is waiting until it's safe enough to come out.

* * *

ONCE THERE WAS A KING (who looked remarkably like your Daddy)

He was born a simple boy,
in a simple land,
but his dreams were bigger than himself.

He dreamed of magical places,
exciting adventures,
and of damsels in distress
                    who needed him.

His simple parents were beside
                    themselves
                    with
                    worry.

"What will become of him?", they asked each
other.
To which neither of them
had an answer.

But the boy was brave
and followed his dreams.
No matter where they
led

him.

By the time he'd grown into a man
he had survived many battles
and defeated all the dragons
and giants
that the world threw at him.

Word of his victories spread
throughout the land
and suddenly strangers wanted to be his friend.

"We must honor this hero!" shouted his new
friends.

So they gave him gifts,
awards,
gold trinkets,
chocolate covered almonds,
and
headaches.

And then they made him a king.

His parents were very proud,
                        and worried no more.
But
some of
these strangers were not really
                        his friends
                        and some
                        meant
                        him
                        harm.

A king's life can be very lonely.

He no longer went off to battle.
There was an army for such things.
He was too precious and (mostly) too well
thought of.
Besides,
there was much to do around the palace.

Like,
signing papers.
Listening to other people's speeches.
Yawning.
Trying to find a pen that worked.

Playing chess.
And looking serious.

His enemies
plotted
to bring him down.
Instead of storming the gates,
they laughed at his jokes,
did everything for him,
patted him on the back,
gave him advice,
and enough rope,
told tall tales,
and complimented him on everything he did.
Which was
now
very little.

After awhile he forgot all about
giants
and dragons

and damsels.

One morning, when he awakened and
rubbed the sleep from his eyes,
                he saw
that his
world
had become
        smaller.

He had become smaller too.
And somehow,
older.

His people worried about him.
He looked so lonely.
"He is dying for an adventure!", said the palace
doctor.
When night
        fell
the king quietly
           packed his bag
and,
disguised as a simple man
crept out of the palace
and
ran
   away.

Far, far, away.

In fact,
he didn't stop running until he reached the
Enchanted Wood
where

it's rumoured
dreams
sometimes
come true.

The Fairy Tree,
which was by far the widest
and
oldest
tree in the forest,
asked the simple man (who was really a king),
what it was he wanted.

The king thought long and hard.
And when he looked up he saw
the most beautiful
damsel
in the world.
She was good,
and kind,
and listened to his stories about his youthful
adventures.

And she didn't yawn once.

One thing led to another
and they were married.
And not long after,
a baby boy was born.

They bought a nice, reasonably priced condo
in the suburbs,
and life
was once again
              simple.

Every night, the man and his son
would watch
adventures
on television.

When the man grew tired
                    and fell asleep
                              in his favourite
chair
in front of the TV set,
the boy and the Mommy
would make sure that
he got to bed as safely as possible.

And when the boy went to sleep
he dreamed
of magical places,
exciting adventures,
and damsels in distress.

His dreams were bigger than himself.

Meanwhile,
in the very next room,
a Daddy dreamed
about the places he'd been,
the dragons he'd tamed,
the giants he'd befriended,
the battles he'd won,
the damsel he loved,
and the warm strong hug of his son.

And
in his sleep,

he smiled.

* * *

FRANK HOWSON

St. Kilda of My Youth

Growing up in Fawkner Street, St. Kilda, was an adventure, as I have written of in the past.

My earliest recollections were of the Barkly Hotel on our street corner. In those days a rough and tumble pub, not helped by the archaic 6pm closing times of the day. That meant that all pubs had to stop serving alcohol by 6 p.m. (can you believe it?) and so men, and women, would rush there from their day jobs and with less than thirty minutes or so would order six or seven or eight pints, line them up and down them in record time. All this did was ensure that there'd be a blood bath outside the pub most nights giving the poor, who couldn't afford to go to Festival Hall and see professional boxing, free front row seats as unhappy drunk patrons settled their imagined differences with their fists. It looked quote poetic on reflection. A kind of slow motion, weird, drunkards dance.

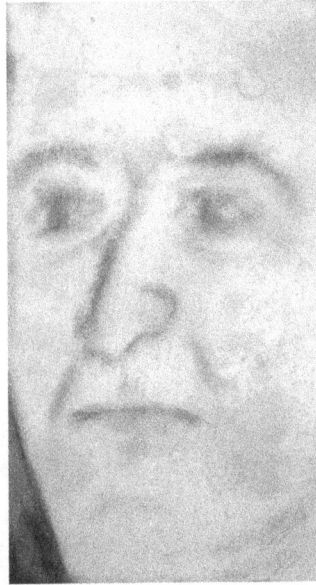

Everywhere there seemed to be street theatre happening.

People falling out of pubs, or pushing to get in before closing time. Children, crying in strollers, waiting for dad or Mum to drink their fill and return to responsibility. Maybe.

Mr. and Mrs. Kilpatrick's Milk Bar was a few doors down and I'd be sent to get supplies for the dinner meal most nights, so I always got a first hand look at the action. Who needed to read "Treasure Island" for thrills when all this was happening outside your door?

My Mum never did a shopping list. She was an improv artist when she cooked. My Dad, who was jockey size, was sent on so many errands he said he'd have been 6'4" if he hadn't run up and down the street so many times at the request of Mum. It usually went something like this ...

"Hey Jack, can you walk up to the Kilpatrick's and get some milk?"

"Is that all you need?" Dad would ask.

"Yes. That'll do."

So off he'd go.

Upon his return he'd be met with ... "Oh. And I need some butter."

At this point he'd look at me with the greatest look of exasperation seen since the great Oliver Hardy.

He'd put the milk down, loudly, on the kitchen table and through tight lips and clenched teeth would again enquire, "Now ... is that all you need?"

"Yes, that'll do me, Jacky," my Mum would assure him. So, off he'd go again. Dutifully walking up the street to ensure we finally got something to eat as our in-house master chef toiled away.

No sooner would he get in the door when he'd hear, "Oh and I could use some more flour too."

I can't repeat what my father's response would be to this. But he certainly made it clear to my Mum what she could do with the dinner.

Who needed television? Every night at my place we had a live comedy sketch worthy of anything Laural & Hardy, Buster Keaton or Chaplin ever did. Maybe that's why it was easy to develop a sense of humour. You had to look at the funny side of things or go mad. Or kill someone. To be totally honest some nights the two of them did attempt the latter but that's a whole other chapter and darker in tone.

Looking back, my upbringing destined me for the theatre. Franz Kafka would've felt right at home at our table. The bizarre was normal to us.

Both my parents were originals. Characters. I have not found their like in anyone else in all my years. Perhaps that's why they were so well loved. They made people laugh, either intentionally or not. When my father died, the crowd couldn't squeeze into St. Colman's Church on Carlisle Street and overflowed onto the pavement outside. Tough men who'd worked with him sobbed like children and tried to explain to me how much he'd meant to them. Didn't they think I knew?

My mother outlived my Dad by more than twenty years so her funeral didn't achieve the same standing-room only crowd but that was only for the simple fact that so many of her friends and family were already gone by then. But the outpouring of grief was just as intense. Many couldn't contemplate a world without Pearl. I must confess that this writer still struggles with it himself.

Being originals meant both of them were irreplaceable.

If my Mum wanted to go and see a romantic film at the classy Victory Theatre my dad would convince her that, while she was enjoying Grace Kelly and Cary Grant act in a story that must've seemed almost science fiction to the world she knew, he'd take me and go see a man's movie at the nearby Memo Theatre. The once beautiful art deco Memo had fallen into disrepair in my youth and I remember my dad affectionately calling it "the Flea Pit." The first such movie outing between us men was "The Creature From The Black Lagoon." I was three years old. I had nightmares for years. Child psychology wasn't a concept in those days. No one ever thought about how things might harm or unnerve a child. You either coped with it ... or harden the fuck up!

Another place I'll always remember was Candy Corner. It was a sublime lolly shop and was situated across the road from Luna Park and the Palais Theatre. When my Mum got a part time job there I thought I was the luckiest kid in the world and was so proud of her. I used to brag about it to my friends. Suddenly I had influence. I was somebody once removed from a somebody. Yep, I learned how powerful it was to have connections. Kids would beg me to accompany them into the shop while they ordered in the hope that my Mum would think they were my pals and give them a very generous serving of their favourites. And she always did. When she lost her job there, perhaps for being over generous, I lost a few friends too. Another life lesson. More grounding for a future in showbiz.

My Dad had been a hurdle jockey, as were his two brothers. One of them, William (Bill) Howson is in the history books for winning several Grand National Steeple Chase races. But my Dad gave it all away when he married so he could get a more reliable job. Did the frustration of that lead to his drinking? Watching his brother go on and become famous and wealthy? Who would know? This was the era when men didn't talk about their problems. Nor acknowledge them. And went to their graves with the secrets of their inner feelings.

He got a job on the St. Kilda Foreshore Council and became a gardener, and a damn fine one. There was nothing he didn't know about plants. He'd walk through a garden and pick various flowers or plants and eat them to impress you. He knew which ones you could eat and which ones would poison you. He was in charge of the O'Donnell Gardens next to Luna Park.

The head of Luna Park in those days was Mr. Keith Marshall, a man I remember looking up to, literally, and being so impressed with the fact that he always wore a suit, collar, tie, and a fedora hat. He dressed like Melvyn Douglas in the movies. Immaculate. After my Mum's tragic demise from a career at Candy Corner, I had a revival in popularity when Mr. Keith Marshall became friends with my dad. It was impossible not to like my father – when he was sober.

I remember Mr. Keith Marshall looking down at me and saying, "Whenever you want free tickets to Luna Park you just go to the front office and tell them you're Jack Howson's son – and that I personally okay however many you want. Alright my boy?"

Oh my God. Now I was bursting with pride about my dad. He had sent me to the top of the popularity charts again. For a kid this was really something. And God aka Mr. Keith Marshall had personally authorized it! I was so happy I could've cried, but I was a St. Kilda kid and possibly still in trauma due to the Creature from the Black Lagoon.

Almost overnight a lot of my friends returned with fanciful excuses for their absence and why they'd dropped me off their birthday party invitations. I must admit, I was becoming a bit cynical about it all.

I spent a lot of my childhood in the O'Donnell Gardens playing Robin Hood, Davy Crockett and Zorro. And rolling down those green hills until I was so dizzy I couldn't stand. It was cheap entertainment. You had to develop an imagination and use it. I always dreamed that one day I'd become so famous and rich that I'd have the powers that be change the name of the O'Donnell Gardens to the Henry (Jack) Howson Gardens in tribute to my dear ol' Dad. That dream still gets me to sleep. Eventually my dad got promoted to boss of the St. Kilda Foreshore, and my Mum always maintained that was his downfall. Now he had no one to answer to and the drinking escalated. It got so bad that my Mum would go and sit in the gardens and watch him in order to cramp his style. This must've humiliated him with his workmates but there you have it. It was a situation that lasted many years and led to World War III being fought every night in our living room.

Most times just verbal brutality, sometimes physical. All I know is I overheard a lot of horrible nasty things that no child has a right to hear. A frightened kid standing at his half opened bedroom door watching and listening to your two heroes destroy each other's ego and pride. And your innocence. So the little boy ran away and hid somewhere inside me.

Some people have remarked that when I laugh or am filled with joy they can actually see the little boy. Maybe it's on those occasions he feels safe enough to come out.

He's still very proud that his mother worked at Candy Corner, and for a time his father was friends with God – the man who ran Luna Park.

* * *

The Spirit of Christmas

Christmas lives in the hearts of children and the child inside us all. It also lives on because of writers such as Francis Church, Irving Berlin (who penned a little ditty called White Christmas), Charles Dickens (in his sublime novel A Christmas Carol), and Frank Capra's screenplay of "It's A Wonderful Life." The latter was a flop at its initial release, but like Christmas it is still with us.

It seems it doesn't much matter whether you tell the story of a pauper child born in a stable, or a jolly chubby white-bearded man in a Coca-Cola suit, or of a husband/father from Bedford Falls who forgets just how many friends he has. The spirit lives on in the telling. This is a true story I heard many years ago, perhaps when I was a child. It touched me then as it touches me now.

On September 21, 1897, the New York Sun published a letter from a young girl named Virginia O'Hanlon. It read ...
Dear Editor, I am eight years old. Some of my little friends say there is no Santa Claus. Papa says, "If you see it in the Sun it's so." Please tell me the truth, is there a Santa Claus?"

One of the paper's editors, Francis Pharcellus Church, decided to rise above the simple question and address the philosophical issues behind it. Church, son of a Baptist minister, had been a war correspondent during the American Civil War, and had witnessed first-hand the great suffering and resultant decline of hope and faith in much of society.

His printed response was so moving that over a century later it remains the most reprinted editorial ever to run in any newspaper in the English language.

It is as follows:

"Yes, Virginia, there is a Santa Claus. He exists as certainly as love and generosity and devotion exists, and you know that they abound and give to your life its highest beauty and joy. Alas! how dreary would be the world if there were no Santa Claus? It would be as dreary as if there were no Virginias. There would be no childlike faith then, no poetry, no romance to make tolerable this existence. We should have no enjoyment, except in sight and sound. The eternal light with which childhood fills the world would be extinguished.

"Not believe in Santa Claus? You might as well not believe in fairies. You might get your papa to hire men to watch in all the chimneys on Christmas eve to catch Santa Claus, but even if you did not see Santa Claus coming down, what would that prove? Nobody sees Santa Claus, but that is no sign that there is no Santa Claus. The most real things in the world are those that neither children nor men can see. Did you ever see fairies dancing on the lawn? Of course not, but that's no proof that they are not there. Nobody can conceive or imagine all the wonders there are unseen and unseeable in the world.

"You tear apart a baby's rattle and see what makes the noise inside, but there is a veil covering the unseen world which not the strongest of men that ever lived could tear apart. Only faith. poetry, love, romance, can push aside that curtain and view and picture the supernal beauty and glory beyond. Is it all real? Ah,

Virginia, in all this world there is nothing else real and abiding.

"No Santa Claus! Thank God! he lives and lives forever. A thousand years from now, Virginia, nay 10,000 years from now, he will continue to make glad the heart of childhood."

And so he does to this day.

For me the spirit of Christmas was the generosity and joy of giving I saw in my mother, Pearl.
Christmas was her favourite time of year and she'd begin shopping for it early January.

I'd always wake early Christmas morning to see a mountain of presents under the tree. Gifts for me, my sisters, my aunts, uncles, cousins, friends, and some mere acquaintances.

We were a working class family and to this day I've no idea how her meager budget stretched to accommodate all those gifts. No doubt she denied herself many things in order to work her miracle. And although we gave her our gifts in return it was not the receiving that mattered to her, but rather the joy of giving. I'll always remember the blissful sparkle in her eyes as she watched us excitedly opening our presents.

Since her death, and my son growing up and away, Christmas is no longer the same for me. It can be a lonely and hollow time for single people. But, come December, I smile in remembrance, because once I was blessed to have witnessed the spirit of Christmas.
It was not found in the gifts. But in my mother's eyes.

* * *

King's Cross

It's easy to be brave when you're young because you're totally naive about the cost to oneself. You also have no idea about mortality and the fragility of life. I guess that's why wars are declared by old men, the decision-makers, but are fought by boys. And now, of course, young women.

Hanging out in Kings Cross was a real eye-opener to a young lad. It felt like Luna Park for grown-ups. All the music pumping out from the bars and nightclubs, the flashing coloured lights, the friendly girls, the drag queens, etc. Of course, once you got over the initial excitement and your eyes adjusted to the lighting show, you glimpsed the circus up close with all its thinly veiled seediness, human despair and danger. Still, to a young guy, away from my home for the first time, it was an adrenaline rush. Illegal casinos, prostitution, organised crime and police corruption were at its height during this era. Heroin had been brought in by American servicemen on leave during the Vietnam war years, and soon became the drug of choice by many Australians. Soon after the major drug rings took its import over and the influx into Sydney of this "product" was huge. Much of these illicit activities were allegedly linked to businessman Abe Saffron, known as "Mr. Sin" or "The

Boss of the Cross." Police were paid off and the most notorious illegal casinos seemed to operate with an impunity. Business was booming and everyone was in on a cut.

I spent many hours in the bars, clubs and strip joints during this time, soaking up the atmosphere and observing how they were run. I guess it was always an interest to me how such places operated. Especially the successful ones. Me and my buddies paid through the nose for drinks so we could sit and be entertained by the, mostly, beautiful strippers. But what's youth if you can't mis-spend it? Meeting these girls in private was an extra negotiation and a frustration for young boys on a limited budget.

While I was coming of age and getting a taste of the night club scene, another young man named John Ibrahim had his sights set on becoming the King of Kings Cross. A Lebanese Australian boy John started out working security for a Cross nightspot but was fueled with an ambition to become the top dog. He worked his way up the ladder learning everything there was to know about the running of successful clubs and making all the right contacts.

At the age of 16, John had witnessed the brother of Bill Bayno, a power broker of the Cross, being attacked by two men and went to his aid. During the ensuing shuffle John received a large knife to his torso. He was rushed to Sydney's St. Vincent's Hospital and placed in a coma for three weeks. Due to the extensive damage to his liver, lungs and intestines, it took John six months to recover. To this day he still bears a large scar from the incident. He was tough, fiercely ambitious, very intelligent and possessed razor sharp instincts about people and situations. Operating in Kings Cross, with the cast of characters who held power at that time, your instincts were your lifeblood. One misjudgment or sloppy decision could get you killed.

By his eighteenth birthday John Ibrahim had acquired a 20% share in his first nightclub, Tunnel Cabaret, By the height of his career it'd be alleged he was involved with a miniMum of 17 clubs in the Cross. The media dubbed him "Teflon John" and "The Teflon Man of Kings Cross" due to his knack of avoiding conviction of any illegal activities.

Eventually we would meet and I found John to be a very charming and savvy man. I was brought up not to pre-judge people on hearsay but rather on how they treated me, and I found John to be a very classy guy. He now manages the career of TV and radio personality Kyle Sandilands.

In the '70s and '80s there seemed to be a very thin line between legal and illegal and this line was usually defined by who your friends were. Corruption in New South Wales was rampant and ran all the way from the cop on the beat to the State government. Certain activities seemed to be in the blind spot of authorities.

One brave journalist, Juanita Nielsen, decided to do something about it by writing a series of expose articles regarding a certain property development in the Kings Cross area. One day she received a call from a gentleman who wanted to have a secret rendezvous so that he could give her some explosive inside information. She kept the appointment but was never seen again. Speculation was that she had been killed and her body put through a meat mincer. A colonial inquest determined that she'd been murdered and the case remains unsolved.

The meat mincer disposal of bodies has long been a favoured solution for the Mafia and other gangland czars. I once asked Chopper Read why he never ate dim sums to which he replied, "I have too much respect for the dead."

One beacon of light in the darkness of the Cross in those years was the Reverend Ted Noffs whose church, The Wayside Chapel, was open 24/7 as a drop-in inn and counselling service to the many itinerants who'd found their way to the Cross only to lose it. He helped save many lives and kept families together, guiding young runaways, as well as drug, drink and gambling casualties back onto a responsible path in life. Although Ted has passed on now his Ted Noffs Foundation still continues today giving a helping hand to those who find themselves in desperate situations.

I was shedding the skin of a young lonely kid and being turned into a man, and the rebirth was at times painful. But that's another story.

* * *

P.F. Sloan

it was the season of youth
when music was sublime and everything was
filled with
wonder
and
possibilities
even for a poor kid who hated school
if the music hadn't saved me
i may've realized how dangerous my future
looked
in the eyes of the realists
and those who suck the joy out of everything
but lennon's voice sneered in their ear

and defended me
and paul sugar coated it
so even
the establishment unwittingly accepted the
revolution
while sweet George
played the guitar breaks that
implanted themselves
in our psyche
ringo conjured up beats
that shouldn't make sense
but made us all want to dance
then a song
"eve of destruction"
came on the radio
and foretold us all
what the truth was
that
there were shadow people
who didn't
dance
and
hell bent on
destroying our world
and us
a brave man must've written
this
song
i feared they would make him pay
and
they did
i looked for his name under the song title
on the record
it was
p.f. sloan

i loved the name
even
and i then after noticed
that he had written
so many songs
that i'd loved
that he must be the fifth beatle?
maybe?
he could've been
thought i
but i was just a kid
and the soundtrack of my life
was being written
by
giants
whose like we wouldn't
much
see again
i even bought his own record
the 45 rpm
p.f. sloan was now in bigger letters on the label
of him singing
his own song
"sins of a family"
on dunhill records
and he warned me again
of the world
and what can happen
to those whose
innocence and light
distance you
from the
shadow makers
and that the
enemy may've even infiltrated

your own
family
but he had said too much
rocked the boat
sang in a voice
that raged
and was defiant
he must be
a communist
said the men of darkness
we can't categorize him
which
makes him a threat
to what we know
and the system
of
counting beans
and labeling tins
and there were others
envious of his talent
and light
and
youth
so the people who gave him to us
eventually took him from us
one of his publicity photos
shows him holding his guitar
as though it's a machine gun
little did I know
he was caught up
in a battle
of a war
that no one wins
then one day
p.f. sloan went away

disappeared
became a mystery
he took something of me with him
that day
i eagerly awaited
his return
checking the writing
credits of every record
just in case
but alas
gone
no more
i waited 40 years for his return
in the meantime
his legend grew
even his protégé
jimmy webb wrote a song for him
about him
"i have been seeking p.f. sloan
but no one knows where he has gone ..."
if jimmy couldn't find him
how could i?
then
one night
in los angeles
when I was lost
and at bazza's place
i surfed the internet
and typed in his name
that magical name
and there he was
we met
we became friends
like it had always
been destined

that we would
we talked
and found
that we had
traveled a similar
road
he had been banished
from the industry for 40 years
me for ten
we were brothers in hurt
and strength
now
every minute i spend with him
inspires
me
enlightens
me
and
even when we
are far apart
half a world away
we
are still connected
in song
in spirit
and
when i think of him
i smile
he
is now back in the world
reborn
with a new album
"my beethoven"
and a new book that explains it all
"what's exactly the matter with me?"

and one night soon
we'll
sit at dan tana's again
over a martini
and without a word
connect
for the world is magic
if you believe
it
so
and
i do

* * *

The Outsiders

When I started making films in Australia it was a time
when "commercial" was a dirty word. Seemed strange to
me because I never set out to make bad films, only ones I
thought more than a few may enjoy. I can't tell you the
resentment hurled at me for having such lofty plans. It
became more than a little bizarre and as a result of the
local critical slaughtering clouded some people's
objective view of my work. I found that my movies
received far greater respect outside of my homeland
which saddened me as I'd always been a staunchly proud
Australian. It compounded my feeling of being an
outsider. Probably not a bad thing for an artist but a
weight nonetheless.

As the years rolled by and I became disenchanted
with my business associates and their agendas my films
turned inward and became more and more personal. A
reflection of my own frustrations and isolation- with a

good dose of anger thrown in for good measure. I had gotten to a place where finally even my harshest critics had to reluctantly admit that, perhaps, I was doing something right, given the overseas acceptance of my work. For example, my family movie "What The Moon Saw" became the first Australian film purchased by Miramax; "Heaven Tonight" the first ever sold to the giant American Broadcasting Corporation; "Hunting" (my directorial debut) sold to Paramount Pictures, etc., etc. Unfortunately, just as I was beginning to have a local critical re-evaluation of my work, my business partner did a few things that gave those with agendas, or just the plain jealous, all the ammunition they needed to justify their ill- feeling.

It took me three years to get rid of my business partner and then another three years to fight him in court. All I had to do at any point during this time, to continue my career and go on making films and money, was to back down and agree to resume my association with him. I did not. As far as moments go it was, integrity-wise, my finest. But, for that shining moment, I lost everything, my home, my family, my money, and all my work. Freedom came at a high price. What followed was 10 years in the wilderness, alone, where I was forced to re-evaluate everything I was or had stood for. There were many times in my anger I cursed how principled

I'd been, given my loss. Would I be as good a man again? I would like to think so, but having lived through the sacrifice and now knowing how high the cost, honestly, I'm not so sure.

Faced with starting again in Australia and having to humbly ask rivals for a job, I decided to go to Los Angeles. I needed a new environment for my mental and physical health. I was in a bad way and had lost a lot of my desire to live. Cutting a creative artist off from his work is like slashing a main artery.

Upon my return to Australia in 2006, I was honoured when Richard Wolstencroft asked me to be President of the Jury at the Melbourne Underground Film Festival. It was indeed a Festival for the Outsiders. The mavericks. People who'd made their movies on their own terms without wilting to the cocktail set of decision makers in the industry. It's the people on the sidelines who kill your boldness. Once you lose your identity and begin making movies for your peers, your voice is lost. And tell me, honestly, how many experts do we have in this country who've ever made a hit film? If they could do it they wouldn't be sitting behind desks being paid a weekly wage to be an industry expert. They'd be out making more hit films wouldn't they?

Over the past six years I've spent a lot of time talking and helping young filmmakers and I couldn't be more proud of them. They don't carry any of the jealous resentment of the closed shop I broke into when I started out. What our industry is paying for now is the fact that the old brigade didn't encourage the next generation. The fat cats just got fatter and as a result our product got thinner. Shame on them. Fortunately, most of them are dead now, or retired, or living in large villas in France from the fortunes they accumulated from making shitty films that didn't get sold anywhere. In most cases not even in their own country.

Oh, and among the healthy signs for the future? Today's young filmmakers don't think "genre" films are a dirty word. To place any style over another is a meaningless and snobbish attitude. The real art comes not in the genre but in how bold and inspired you can be working within those restrictions. So, I salute all the brave, new, original outsiders who are finding their own voice and way in the current film industry. I salute their talent, their guts and lead the applause in their honour. They inspire me to be better.

* * *

Thank You and Good Night

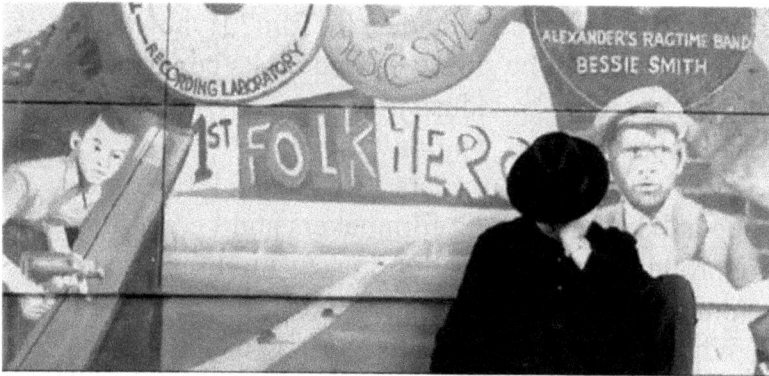

Somewhere along the way it changed. Were we sleeping? Or merely so preoccupied filling our lives with crap we didn't notice. Perhaps it took place over a very long period of time, just an inch a day, not enough to see until it was done. But whatever. The result was the same.

One day we awakened to find the old world gone – that place of unbiased reporting.

I always remember an old editor I met in my youth who'd spent his entire life in the newspaper business. He barked orders while chain smoking several packs a day, a bottle of scotch in his bottom drawer. His gospel was simple – "just give me the facts, not your opinion. Don't treat the reader like an idiot. If you stick to the facts, and nothing but, they'll work it out for themselves."

He probably wouldn't have much time for an opinion piece such as I am writing now. But there used to be a difference between the news and opinion pieces. Alas, no more. For some time now, especially during my nine years of living in Los Angeles, I could pick up any newspaper and within reading a few paragraphs tell you which party the reporter voted for. I admire people with strong political beliefs because I, terminally disillusioned and disappointed, have none. Maybe I haven't believed in anyone since those three shots in Dallas. Or perhaps it was Bobby. The sacking of Whitlam? Or the roll call of Prime Ministers and Presidents that have sold us out to get re- elected. Anyway, in the words of Paul Anka's song made famous by the late, great Buddy Holly, "I guess it doesn't matter anymore."

But, as I was saying, somewhere along the line we lost the news and gained the views. Nothing irritates me more than reading what should be an unbiased, unemotional, dry account of the facts and suddenly realising I'm being manipulated. Some reporter is following party lines to slant a story for a specific effect. Forget that there may be real lives caught up in this zealous exercise. Don't get me wrong. I love reading opinion pieces – especially if I admire the person whose opinion it is – but when it infiltrates into Page One news

– or headlines – it becomes something else. Something sinister.

I've read headlines that have damned people only to find a convenient about-face in the final paragraph, if you get that far, that covers the writer's arse against legal action. They rely on us busy people running hatless through life not having enough time to read anything but the headline. And so, at the water cooler or at the coffee shop, or on the iPhone, the misinformation becomes fact. "Do you know ...?" or "I've heard ..."

Yes, folks, Judas is in the small print. And the Chinese Whispers. We have been betrayed by those who swore an ethical oath to tell the truth, the whole truth and nothing but. We are now lumbered in two categories – the great misinformed, or those stricken with the disease of indifference.

The latter has swept the world more thoroughly than any disease since we crawled out of the Great Swamp or got kicked out of the Garden of Eden (depending on your view of evolution).

Goebbels, the master publicist, believed if you told the Big Lie enough times it became fact. And so it has. Tragically, if Mr. Goebbels was a young man today he'd be working for newspapers, tapping phones and murdering people in print.

Either that or Head of Marketing at Paramount Pictures.

* * *

We Can Be Heroes (For Just One Day)

It's no secret – we have always craved heroes. The loner who steps forth and willingly lays down their life so that others may live. Call them Jesus, Davy Crockett, Sherlock Holmes, Joan of Arc, Sydney Carton, Gandhi, etc., etc., etc. Like the gestation of a pearl, our heroes are formed as a defense mechanism against a threatening irritant. No one is born a hero. They are made. In the words of John Wayne, "Courage is being scared to death – but saddling up anyway." Few of us know what we'd do in a life or death moment – that split second decision to stand or flee. As illustrated in Stephen Crane's masterpiece novel "The Red Badge of Courage" that split second decision will mark us forever as either coward or hero. I wonder how many cowards crave to return to that defining moment – and this time

lay down their life in lieu of the hell of regret and shame they have since endured.

Heroes, genuine ones, are hard to come by. In fact, the times we live in seem to rarely throw them up anymore. Hence the media and movies invent them for us so we can glow and feel safe in the knowledge that giants still do walk amongst us.

But in our eagerness to find heroes we are continually disappointed at being sold snake oil. Let's face it, there are only two types of stories that sell newspapers and magazines – the first one is to build 'em up, the second – to tear 'em down. The perfect example is Princess Diana who started out as the media's "darling who could do no wrong" and ended up their punching bag, stalked to death. I also remember when Alan Bond was hailed a hero. And Paul Hogan. And et finitum.

The real heroes mostly go unnoticed by the press. They probably aren't photogenic anyway. They are the battlers who work themselves to an early grave so that their kids are fed and clothed; or the person who ruins a career rather than continue to make money out of a lie; and the firemen who run into a building when everyone else is running out.

Todd Beamer was an airline passenger travelling on 9/11 when he found himself on a hi-jacked plane heading toward the White House. After initially being terrified, he summoned the courage and the support of a few other passengers by uttering the words, "Let's roll!" broke open the cockpit door with a food cart, overpowered the terrorists and veered United Airlines Flight 93 off its intended target, straight into a field in Pennsylvania. Ordinary people swallowing their fear, and thought of themselves, for the greater good of others. Which brings me to Julian Assange.

Remember how excited we were in 1974 that two reporters from the Washington Post could bring down the President of America? We loved it because we didn't much like Nixon. He looked creepy. Had a five o'clock shadow year in, year out, and hadn't ended an unpopular war that spilled into our living rooms every night ruining dinner. What looked like a victory for freedom to us back in '74 has, in my opinion, created an even bigger monster. Now the press feel they are entitled to know everything about all of us and report it if they think it's newsworthy. In this new age of no boundaries there are no such things as private lives anymore. Perhaps there's a connection here as to why there're so few heroes around? What complex person can have their private life scrutinised and come out a saint? We have all made mistakes (hopefully learned from them), trusted the wrong people, behaved badly, been divorced, been angry, been down, been bruised. But isn't all that stuff the sand that makes the irritation that makes the pearl? Would J.F.K have been so well thought of if we'd known all the aspects of his private life? Would it have made a difference to what we thought of his work as President? Should it?

Did it matter that Graham Kennedy was gay? Surely all he owed us was a brilliant performance every weeknight? And did he not deliver that in abundance? Did it matter that Churchill could be a belligerent drunk bully at times? My point is this – there are some things the public don't have the right to know. Nor need to.

Is it a good thing that some of the secret information Julian Assange released to the world is out there? Probably. Does all of it deserve to be public? Probably not. But who decides about this? If I were to approve secret documents to be released it may not correlate with what you want made public, or the next person. So, don't we vote into power political parties to make those judgment calls? And if we don't like their decisions isn't it our right, nay our duty, to vote them out?

One has to question the responsibility of releasing secret documents about Afghanistan. Why? Because we are, like it or not, involved in a war. A long and bloody war that has taken the lives of many and still it goes on. Do I want the US and Allied Forces (including us) to win this war? Well, if the alternative is the Taliban, you bet your arse.

One could not have had a more liberal President than Franklin D. Roosevelt. The new deal guy. A man who clearly cared about the people. He was reluctant to enter a war but when Pearl Harbour was bombed he didn't have much of a choice. Yet how would President Roosevelt have responded to someone releasing his secret documents and information to the world (and his enemies) during wartime? I have no doubt he would've had the culprit charged with treason and made to pay the penalty for such. Thankfully it didn't happen and the outcome of the war was not altered.

But to give blanket approval to Julian Assange's actions is to open a can of worms that may never be closed again.

I was living in Los Angeles during 9/11 and saw the subsequent televised war in Afghanistan. On CNN one day I watched one of Geraldo Rivera's reports from the war zone. During it he actually drew a diagram in the sand and pointed out where the US forces were secretly based and went on to expound what their plan of attack was. He obviously didn't think Osama Bin Ladin watched CNN. Not one of Geraldo's shining moments. I'm not sure how many of his countrymen he put at risk. But even one was too many.

Let me remind us all we are involved in a war. Whether you agree with that war or not, is another matter. But to put our young men and women's lives at risk is an act of astounding stupidity. And not my kind of hero.

* * *

The Director

To express life you must first have experienced it in all its beauty, ugliness, rejection, innocence, debauchery, brutal truth and the sweetness of a child's smile. It pays to have experienced everything but death although that continually holds its own fascination which you toy with on a daily basis. You tease it as much as it teases you, neither of you flinching. For to be an artist that may be remembered past evening you have to be bold. Take chances. Not afraid to be laughed at, ridiculed, scorned, and stabbed in the back by the arrogant ignorant who will ignore your finest work but spread the word night and day about your missteps. You will learn to measure your success on the level of resentment in some circles. They will say you are mad – and the truth is you probably are. For you are going out on a limb, endeavoring to push further to find that magic moment of truth at the expense of formula, tried-and-true tricks, imitation,

rewards, and anything phony. This cross will make you feel constantly alone in a room of people looking at you waiting for answers, and the easy option. Although you have by now a tough exterior and pretend their lack of faith doesn't hurt, your heart records every scar. You notice everything. It's your job. It's your curse. The depth of how much you care will become the depth of your pain. You have been praised by giants yet the scornful snicker of a chorus girl gets to you. If what you achieve is brilliant, then many will claim the credit. If you stumble you'll stumble alone. No friend in sight. There is always that assassin in the corner playing cards pretending he is not there to take your life. He eventually will but even that will make you smile as you experience the final secret and the regret that you almost achieved the reproduction of it in front of lights and the monster with a thousand eyes, the audience. Even the sharpest critics will not be able to tell how close you came. But you will know. And smile that it really didn't matter to anyone else but you.

* * *

THE WRITER

The typewriter insulted my mother.
Your recent publication of my work got me
ridiculed.
The critics sent my champagne back after
spitting in it.
Thank God my father
died, I have been using
his name.
This room has killed
me.
I had a heart bursting
with love for humanity
until that bloody
transplant. I think they
gave me yours.
This paper smells.
The vodka knows my ex-wife and has been
phoning her late at night.
My recent suicide has been called a publicity
stunt.
Women scattered my ashes in a dumpster after
cursing my existence.
My obit was written by a fool who can't spell. He
normally covers amateur football. The eulogy at
my funeral consisted of the reading of a
financial report detailing how much money I
owe friends.
They tell me my work has amounted to nothing
and I'll only be remembered as a suspect in an
ongoing murder investigation.

Maybe I could've found love if only I'd left this
room. But where would I have gone with it? I
don't think I'll come back. I need to talk to God.

* * *

THE ONLY SON

There's the room, second to the left
Just down the hallway before the light
From the window throws everything into a blur
Like my memory
Of that house where my father fought
World World Three every night
The only survivors of that holocaust
My sisters and I
Sometimes I stumble back
Into the land of what may have been
Through those fields of strikes
And ambitions run out before their time
The only son
In the empty stadium
The bleachers filled with ghosts
Each one an expert on the game
Their hearts broken, their heroes gone
On the wind their mothers' voices
Calling them home before dark

* * *

Political Correctness

Political Correctness has pretty much killed humour. There are now whole areas of human behaviour and difference that can no longer be commented upon lest one risk the chance of being blacklisted. No pun intended. I was brought up to believe Senator Joe McCarthy was a bad man. But, ironically, his ghost is alive and well and seemingly stronger than ever.

There was one comedian, or social commentator, Lenny Bruce, who literally paid with his life for daring to push down the walls of conservatism by shining a spotlight on the absurdity and hypocrisy of it all. His legacy survived for a few decades and passed the torch onto such comedians as Bill Hicks, George Carlin, Richard Pryor, Joan Rivers, Sam Kinison, Bill Cosby, Eddie Murphy, Robin Williams, and others. Having recently watched the brilliant Bob Fosse film "Lenny" starring Dustin Hoffman, in another extraordinary performance playing Lenny Bruce, I'm not sure Lenny wouldn't be crucified all over again if he was around today.

Thank God there is Ricky Gervais and Larry David that are brave enough to walk the tightrope of what is acceptable, although watching their balancing act can sometimes be nerve wracking hoping they don't over-reach and we lose two more brilliant and insightful social commentators. To paraphrase Lenny Bruce in his plea to the judge who bankrupted him and thus rendered him a death sentence, "Don't you see? You need madmen like me to tell you when you're running off the rails!" But it was Lenny who was run off the rails and into a ditch of which he could not conceive ever scrambling out of. In the words of Bob Dylan, lamenting in song the death of Lenny Bruce, (all he did was) "... to show the wise men of his day to be nothing more than fools."

But, sadly, the fools have multiplied and are back in power. They have invented a term called "Political Correctness" that has effectively silenced free speech. Although I'm not convinced speech was ever free of repercussions. It has made it near impossible to have healthy debate or raise a lateral voice to present a new radical idea. Imagine the trouble John Lennon, always one to ridicule tin gods with the sometimes hurtful truth, would find himself in these days?

All political correctness does is hide the bigots. It doesn't make them go away, it merely allows them to shield themselves behind the presently acceptable choice of slogans. I, on the other hand, side with free speech. If there are nasty-minded people out there I want them to have the public forum to expose themselves. I certainly don't want them blacklisted, or jailed, or fined either – isn't it enough that we know who they are and what their agendas are?

I am surprised at how many people violently oppose censorship and yet support political correctness. Isn't it one and the same, or am I stupid?

Joan Rivers believed nothing was off limits when it came to comedy. But she didn't just dish it out, she took it too. Even making a joke of her own late husband's suicide that had devastated her. Humour can sometimes, in the hand of the great comics, illuminate things, clarify, show up the absurdity of the situation and diffuse the pain by laughing at it – and thus commence the healing.

I'm not one for categorizing people, placing them in boxes with identifiable tags, etc., we are all much too complex for that. I guess for that reason I have never been a racist. I don't think in terms of colour when I meet someone, but rather by the fibre of the person's inner soul and their guiding integrity. Once, when I was living in Los Angeles, one of my African-American friends said to me one night, "You know the reason we like you? We don't detect any attitude."

I replied, "Well I came from a working class background and lived in a suburb where there were many different nationalities. I leaned very quickly that there are only two races of people on this earth – good people and assholes! And every race has 'em."

We both laughed and my friend said, "You're a hundred per cent right."

It's like the old joke, "When I was growing up I was so poor I thought I was black!" Boom boom. Humour, yes. But also true.

Ignorance is the root cause of bigotry and prejudice. The more you mix with different races the more you see that we're all the same – the family of man – with the same worries, the same concerns, the same insecurities, the same flaws, the same pressures to achieve, the same capacity for love and forgiveness.

And most races have been slaves to another at various times through history. I have Irish ancestry and they of course were slaves to the English for several centuries. Even being denied the right to learn to read and write in case they became too knowledgeable. Yet, isn't it interesting how adversity can eventually become a gift? Many believe that because the Irish weren't allowed to read and write that's why they became such great storytellers. Their only way of communicating was to stand on a street corner and tell their story, or hold court in a pub for anyone who'd listen. Or turn it into a song and sing it. Do I hold resentment to the English for what they did to generations of my ancestors? No. The past is dead and so are you if you live in it. Or may as well be.

I'm glad that Hollywood has at long last started making films like "The Book Thief" that shows that not all Germans were Nazis. And that many, many Germans, not just Schindler, helped save Jewish lives for the simple reason that it was wrong. Many other Germans who opposed Hitler coming to power paid with their lives once he did. That is fact.

Abraham Lincoln was a white man. He saw wrong and he tried to right it. In doing so, he eventually paid with his life. And in the sixteen hours of his agonizing death I hope he at least had the comfort of knowing he'd truly achieved something and his life had made a difference. Did he do it out of political correctness? No. It was a very unpopular stand to take at the time and many, including Lincoln himself, were surprised when he was voted in for a second term as President. Perhaps the public, always smarter than we give them credit for, sensed it was the just thing to do. But it would not have happened had there not been free speech and very vigorous public debate. Were politically incorrect things said during that campaign? Of course, and the perpetrators were exposed for what they were. Just about every race in the world has another race that they like to kick around. I guess it makes them feel bigger. It is staggering how old mankind is and yet, some, still have a problem with the shade of another's skin. It is truly heartbreaking how little we have evolved if that is still an issue.

There was a cartoon recently that depicted the recent boat people dilemma. It showed a group of aboriginals on the beach watching Captain Cook's ship approaching. The caption was "Look what happened when we allowed boat people to land!"

Again, humour highlights the absurdity and hypocrisy of a very dramatic and hotly contested situation.

There was a Jewish woman in L.A who told me she objected to being called a "Jew" and that it was racist. I must've looked a little confused because she then said, "Don't you agree it's horrible?"

I suppose having listened to too much Lenny Bruce, I replied, "But it's just a word. An abbreviation. It's like me being called an "Aussie" – isn't it?"

I tried to explain that with any of the politically incorrect words that, to me, it's not the word that's offensive, but rather the tone. If I'm called an Aussie in a friendly or humorous tone why would I get upset? If, on the other hand, it's said with a tone of sarcasm or ridicule, then it's a whole different matter.

I know people who've destroyed their careers by using the "N" word. Yet African-Americans can call each other that and get away with it. Why? Because it's said in a friendly and humorous way. It's all about the tone. I was saddened when I heard that there was a PC push to have Mark Twain's masterpiece, "The Adventures of Huckleberry Finn" rewritten to have the "N" word removed. This is political correctness gone mad. We are talking about what is arguably one of the greatest American novels ever written, if not the greatest. The word is used in it because at the time of the novel ... well ... that's how people spoke. And not always in an unfriendly manner. Huck himself uses it to talk to his slave friend. The point I'm trying to make is, if we start rewriting history we are all doomed, for "he who does not learn from the past is destined to repeat it."

You can't get away with calling any nationality anything derogatory and that's a good thing. Oh, hold on, you can call poor white people "white trash" and get away with it. No one will sue you, no one will blacklist you, and no one will banish you from respectable society. Doesn't seem fair in a time when we are all trying to be equal and granted some common respect. At the end of the day isn't it about humanity?

I was sitting at the bar of a restaurant in Santa Monica once when a very classy looking couple, not sure what their nationality was, asked the Mexican busboy what type of bread the restaurant served.

The busboy answered, "White bread."

The dark complexioned gentleman customer replied, "I am offended by your comment."

The very confused busboy came over to me and asked how he should describe the bread in future. I told him the problem was not with him, but rather the customer. Some will find offense with anything. And do.

There is also a PC push to rewrite one of the gospels in the New Testament where a Jewish voice in the crowd yells out at the trial of Jesus, to "Crucify him and let his blood be on our hands and that of our children!"

Well I wasn't there, and ironically neither was the writer, but how that one comment from some bozo in the audience can label all Jewish people as "Christ killers" baffles me. To set the record straight, the majority of Jewish people actually seemed to like Jesus. Some even loved him. Otherwise who were all those thousands who came to hear him speak, or welcomed him into Jerusalem putting palms at the feet of his donkey to make a trail? The death of Jesus was purely political. The High Priest Caiphas was in the pocket of the Romans, one only needs to see the lavish palace the Romans gave him to prove that, and Jesus was hell bent on forcing a public confrontation with Caiphas, whom he called the "Old Fox," to expose him as a fraud who had sold his people out.

Of course, given that scenario there was only going to be one outcome – Caiaphas was going to protect his job at any price. Even if it took the death of a trouble maker from his own tribe. But blaming all Jewish people forevermore for this is absurdity in the highest order. It would be like blaming all Americans for what Senator Joe McCarthy did. It wasn't personal. It was purely political. Was Jesus the son of God? Or a messenger sent to reveal things to us? That's a whole different discussion and healthy debate.

But make no mistake, his death was political and benefited the few in power, not the many people on the street who seemed to enjoy Jesus' morality tales about loving each other and being the best of who we could be. What is there not to like? From all reports Jesus was a very devout Jew and a very fine rabbi. And it's a shame that there's been a divide between Jesus and his own people, whom he obviously loved enough to stand up over a principle because he felt they were being sold short.

Which brings me to Mel Gibson and what happened one drunken night on a road in Malibu. Mel, driving home after having had too many drinks to celebrate the completion of his latest directorial film "Apocalypto," was pulled over by a cop doing his duty. Mel, being pie-eyed and not the happiest of drunks, asked the cop, "Are you Jewish?" When the cop replied in the affirmative he was subjected to some horrible and nasty racist remarks that no one with any decency can condone.

But, having been the child of an alcoholic father, I know full well how vile and nasty drunks can be when they want to lash out. With my father nothing was off limits and no vulnerability was protected when you were in his sights. I have often said about him that, "He was the nicest man in the world – up to ten drinks. After that, he'd wander the house looking for someone to blame."

Did he mean what he said when he was drunk? Of course not. I know that for a fact because I saw his pathetic sober remorsefulness the next morning when he couldn't understand why no one was talking to him. But when he was drunk, he would say anything to hurt you. Anything. Anything to make you feel as bad as he obviously did. Hurt people hurt people.

I have no doubt that if the cop that stopped Mel had've been African- American it would've been a tirade against black people. Or if the cop had've been Mexican – Mexicans. Or Irish. Or English. Or Australian. Or Muslim. Or whatever. We are talking about an alcoholic who was obviously in need of help. And anger management classes. Mel did wrong. He shamed himself. But did he deserve to be blacklisted for 10 years? You answer that.

Recently a female Jewish reporter wrote an article defending Mel. She stated that at the time, like most people, she had gone from loving to hating him when he made those anti-Semitic remarks. But she said that some years later, during his banishment, she got to know him and found him to be a very caring and kind human being and that she genuinely didn't believe he was a racist. No, he was a nasty tongued alcoholic. She also revealed that Mel has many Jewish friends and has helped many Jewish causes on the basis that it not be publicized. He tried to help Courtney Love when she was on a road to self-destruction and no one else cared. He rescued Britney Spears when the poor girl was obviously having a breakdown on live television and the rest of the world seemed content to watch and enjoy her disintegration every night on the 6 o'clock news. And Robert Downey Jr. credits Mel with not just saving his career, but his life. Downey has publicly stated, "Isn't it sad that a man who had secretly helped so many people in their time of trouble, has been deserted in his." The female reporter in her defense of Mel stated that he has paid dearly for his undeniably bad behavior. Ten years in the wilderness. Ten years out of what had been a distinguished career. Surely he has paid in full? It seems to me that the basis of most religions is forgiveness and the power of redemption. Do people deserve a second chance? I would like to believe so. If not, why do we send people to jail and waste all that money housing them if it is not in the name of rehabilitation? You do the crime, you do the time. Otherwise, if we're not going to forgive, we may as well kill people when they do something wrong and save all that money. If we don't grant a second chance in society, then they are dead anyway.

Political correctness? Surely we are grown ups and can self regulate ourselves. If not, we'll be exposed for who we are. And isn't that a good thing? Well it is as long as we are open to forgive and applaud someone who makes the effort to admit to a mistake, as well as put the effort into working on becoming a better person. It always irritates me when I hear someone calling someone a "Nazi" just because they have an opposing idea or a different political leaning to us. Some of these people who call others such things will be the first to tell you they are politically correct. Well, as long as you agree with them that is. To call someone a "Nazi" is to either be grossly over-exaggerating what they have done – or else making light of what the real Nazis did. And that, my friends, would be an unjust and dangerous thing to do.

Although some people at times may say things that irritate us, or offend, or hurt, I believe we still have to defend the bigger concept of free speech. Once you start censoring or restricting it in any way you end up losing more than you gain.

I have been in show business since I was a boy and over that time have probably been called just about everything hurtful you can imagine. I have also been praised, thankfully, on occasion. It comes with the territory and hardens you to abuse from uninformed, ignorant or just plain envious people – "sticks and stones may break my bones but words will never harm me." Let the hurtful (hurt) ones amongst us reveal themselves and we can avoid their company in the future. Life goes on. And so do we. Hopefully wiser and more discriminating as to who we let in our lives.

When people call others nasty names they don't belittle you. They belittle themselves.

Go in peace and try to find the best in others regardless of their race, nationality, religious or political belief. It will also help you find the best in you.

* * *

A New Year Prayer

As we embark upon a new year - let us strive to be kinder, more patient, more grateful for the small acts of generosity (that happen every day if we stop to notice), wiser, more understanding, true hearted, less controlling of things that cannot be controlled (this includes other people), loving, less ignorant, slower to rush to judgment, peaceful and joyous. We are here but once so let us not waste time by dwelling on our past battles and resultant scars, but rather rejoice in still being here to awaken each day. It is indeed a gift. And an opportunity. Appreciate it.

* * *

R.I.P

Killed by the slow moving internet connection.
Killed by the small print.
Killed by the waiting.
Killed by the people who never showed up.
Killed by the opportunities lost.
Killed by never being fully understood.
Killed by the loss of parents.
Killed by the orphanage.
Killed by never finding your way home again.
Killed by too much false love.
Killed by too many people asking how you are but not wanting the answer.
Killed by being too honest.
Killed by too many battles fought alone.
Killed by reading between the lines.
Killed in your sleep.
Killed by the mediocre.
Killed by finding out too much.
Killed by never finding yourself.
Killed by the dull-eyed crowd.
Killed by giving more than you had.
Killed by the slow cooker.
Killed by critics who only enjoy sport.

Killed by gossip.
Killed by pacifists smelling blood.
Killed by mistake.

* * *

Eulogy of Alex Scott

The most precious things in the world are those things
that are irreplaceable in our lives. We are gathered here
today to say farewell to one. Irreplaceable in his talent.
Irreplaceable
in our hearts.
Irreplaceable
in his truth.
There's a lyric
in a Jackson
Browne song
that says,
"Does it take a
death to learn what a life is worth?" No. Not in this case.
I think we were all aware at every stage just what Alex
Scott was worth in our lives. I will miss that golden
voice that could even make the reading of the telephone
book sound profound. I will miss his shining talent that I
was honoured to have witnessed in full flight. But most
of all I'll miss his friendship. His smile. His wicked
sense of humour. The twinkle in his eye. His thoughts.
His priceless stories. The look on his face when he
listened to Beethoven. And that laugh that I was
fortunate enough to capture on film. I will also miss his
honesty. In this business of show where people tell you
what they think you want to hear, and then distort the
facts behind your back, Alex was a beacon of truth. If
you received a compliment from him, you knew he

meant it. I was fortunate to have received a very big compliment from him about a film I'd done. I still bask in that glow. But, perhaps to balance me, at the screening of my next project he told me, in his most measured tones, that he felt it was "a piece of shit".

To paraphrase that lyric again, "There's no way I could tell you what he meant to me."

Perhaps his most fitting epitaph is written in the words of Antony lamenting the death of Marcus Brutus. "This was the noblest Roman of them all. His life was gentle, and the elements so mixed in him that nature might stand up and say to all the world: "This was a man!" Recently, there was a funeral for the preacher who, along with the members of his Bible reading class, was the victim of another senseless gun spree in the U.S. and President Obama attended to eulogise him. To paraphrase – he said – "I could spend a lot of time listing this man's triumphs, noting his awards, his acts of kindness, naming the many whose lives were changed due to his compassion. But – perhaps there is no greater accolade than the following – This was a good man. And he lived a good life. And we are better for having known him." Rest in peace, dear Alex.

Good night, sweet prince. I'm going to miss you every day.

* * *

In Defence of God

Imagine, if you will, eternity in darkness and with darkness all there is in front of you. That was God's lot in life. Those of you who've experienced short periods of meditation may be able to grasp just how chilled and cool God is. Sometimes His mind can wander for centuries. He apologises profusely for any inconvenience this caused during the Spanish Inquisition and the Crusades.

Anyway, at some point during an eternity of darkness and nothingness, God got really bored. Really bored. So bored He created stars. Diamond pinholes in eternal night. Some of them he gave names to like DaVinci, Beethoven, Lincoln, Chaplin, Welles, Tesla, Bell, Hawking, Turan, Picasso, Einstein, Elvis, Beatles, Dylan – oh, and Kanye West.

When interviewed by Neale Donald Walsch, God stated that His "... greatest creation was free will." He gave it to us as His gift to make our own way through the darkness as best we could and to experience, in a smaller way, the joy He experienced in creating something from scratch. Trouble is, He said, "... although I've given you complete freedom to make your own decisions, as soon as something goes wrong, you blame me!" God is now in therapy thanks to us. And, like a poor person, His only option for therapy is to talk to Himself. Sometimes in that magic hour, in the silence just before dawn, if you listen closely you may hear Him.

In the story of Cain and Abel the story symbolizes what would happen if God favoured one child over another. The result of this was the creation of envy. And from that, murder. Human kind took to the latter like a duck to water and even governments adopted it on a large scale as the final solution to any threatening problem.

There are many ways to murder someone. You can either take their life in the Biblical sense or there's the more modern subtle way of assassinating someone by lies and innuendo which has been favoured by the print press. And bitter editors.

When asked why He invented suffering, He replied, "It is necessary to pass through hell before you can fully appreciate heaven."

During that same interview He, a little impatiently, addressed the concern regarding apathy and boredom for those of us who toil in the wastelands, "Look, I gave you music, Hollywood movies and Bob Dylan didn't I? You think you're bored, try living alone in total darkness for eternity!"

Yes, He has lost his patience with us on many occasions. Read the Old Testament and you will find a God who, like all youth, is angry, impatient, revengeful, and quick to judge. By the New Testament we have an older, more understanding God who's able to look past our ignorant mistakes and see the bigger picture. He sent His son to herald this new age and inform us of the change but unfortunately there were those amongst us who weren't ready for the outrageous and highly controversial concept that "we should all love each other and try to get along for the betterment of all," and they killed him. God has sent us many other messengers in the years since who've attempted to give us the same message, ie., Gandhi, Martin Luther King, John Lennon, etc., but, unfortunately, we killed them too. It seems if you preach hate you're as safe as milk and will die in your bed of old age. But have the audacity to peddle love and understanding and your days are numbered.

This loss of his own son caused God to withdraw from the world and to distance Himself from us. It is indeed revealing that ensuing visions brought to us messages from the other world tend to be in the form of Mary. Not Jesus. And, just like a woman, she still attempts to see the best in us and loves us despite our flaws and hurtful actions. The miracle of unconditional love. Jesus, on the other hand, thinks we're a bunch of idiots with a thirst for blood who haven't learnt a thing from the past 2,000 years, or his death. Word has it he has given up on us and spends most of his time gardening.

For those amongst us who hate God because they didn't get what they wanted for Christmas, spare a thought for His suffering. He has been alone for eternity, living in darkness with no one to love. Knowing full well what it was like to feel like an orphan, God gave birth to a huge family and tried to make a home for us. He now knows the pain of having had that family, in main, disown, slander, and hate their father for being the cause of their existence.

Perhaps that is why God created a miracle called forgiveness. He lives in the hope that we will all find it. As He has.

When asked if He ever worried about our future, He replied, "No. Not at all. I worry about your present but never the future for I know the outcome and what, ultimately, awaits you. You see, at the end of your journey all roads lead to me. And, like any parent that loves their child, regardless of what you've done, you are greeted with forgiveness and abundant, unconditional love, understanding, and welcomed home."

Jesus, on the other hand, may take some time to warm to you.

* * *

Last Word on P.F. Sloan

I am heartbroken to wake to the news that one of my dearest friends in the world, the extraordinary songwriter/singer and even more extraordinary human being, passed away last night. I had planned to go to L.A and spend Christmas with him but God had other plans and we'll now have to wait some time to meet up again. Words cannot express what that man meant to me so I won't try and stumble through them as it would only come up short.

What happened to Phil in his professional life was unfair and the people of darkness silenced a voice of genius at the peak of his career and took him from the world for 40 years. But those people passed and Phil came back with a superb comeback album called "Sailover" that is a gift to anyone who bought it and contains new versions of some of his greatest hits plus new insights into life and God's grace. And now Phil has passed.

The last time I saw P.F. Sloan was in L.A earlier this year when I'd travelled there for the memorial of another dear friend of mine Rick Rosas. Phil and I caught up on my second last day in town and it was a joyous meeting. We had both missed each other so much and all we did was laugh and joke and tell stories all afternoon while we feasted on hamburgers and hotdogs at Pink's Diner in L.A., oh and got told off for smoking in the outdoor smoking area by a woman who was obviously so concerned about her lungs she chose to live in Los Angeles!

Anyway, I will treasure that time and when I think of it, and him, I will smile. I think the greatest thing you can say about someone is that by knowing them I became a better person. Such was Phil's spirit. I was blessed that he appears in my film "Remembering Nigel" and was such a supporter of its message that he chose to write the incidental music score for it. All that remains of him now are the songs and music of his life. And the glorious memories he has given all those who opened their hearts to him. I guess a part of you dies with every close friend who passes, because they take with them the part you reserved for them in your heart. Today I feel a big part of me is gone. Farewell, dear friend, you are now safe from this sometimes cruel world. His passing reminds me of the words of Don McLean in his heartfelt tribute to another gentle soul, Vincent Van Gogh, "... this world was never made for one as beautiful as you."

* * *

Andre

(Inspired by the short life of Holocaust victim Georges
Andre Kohn.)

I wish you could've seen today
The sun was out
And the warmth made you feel
That the world was safe
I wish you could've touched my hand
And known for sure
That the darkness was gone
And the good guys won
I wish you could've looked away
And never seen
All the shadow people in their uniforms
I wish I could've saved your life
I wish...
I wish...

I have a photograph of you smiling
Happy as a child
Captured in a frame
Perfect light
Before the dark clouds came...

I wish you could've seen to day
The sun was out
And the warmth made you feel
That the world was safe
I wish you could've touched my hand

And known for sure
That the darkness was gone
And the good guys won

I wish you could've seen today
The sun was out, Andre
And the world was safe...
Today

* * *

Gone

i see my own ghost
standing with the soldiers on
your doorstep

i can't conceal my corpse smile

in this shanty town of dead—end
streets
i feel like napoleon in defeat
you built me up just to knock me
down

didn't you?in this hungry lawless
town
the women are vampires
and the men broken in spirit

                    fugitives
                    from
                    themselves
                    confused
                    as to how
                    to act
                    anymore
or what is wanted of them

suffer, little children
the fire will forge your way
i see a white sky
but blue is your colour
swirling blue
this mood suits you
take it and clothe yourself

somewhere in your heart
miles davis plays

i would've put you in my book
if you'd put me in yours
it would've been nice to have been
remembered
in something

i would've written you just right

but alas

my sorrow runs into dawn
and death is just a sleep
sweet dreams, dear one
this night will be long
and you'll not wake
to anymore
cold

hard
stares

instead
tonight
you'll sleep and dream of beauty

could you please return all the
things i left unsaid?

where's our shapeless and misty
future
now?

gone, my friend
gone
gone like the cowboys
gone like the old west
gone like your faded comic books
gone like you

sorrow
crying
brooding
withering
as daylight goes

the voice of my heart is cracked
and trembling

i have uncovered the meaning of
everything
which is
nothing

your word was once my law
now I have no code to live by
nothing to believe in
all my heroes are dead
dinner is ruined

time ran out
and the voices in my head were
wrong

having sold my life story to
someone for a song

I can no longer reminisce
without the risk of infringing
someone's copyright

preparations are being made for
the last hurrah

About the Author

FRANK HOWSON

Frank Howson is an international award winning film & theatre director/playwright/screenwriter/producer. The first film he produced and wrote was the AFI award winning "Boulevard of Broken Dreams" that has since become an Australian classic. Other film he produced and wrote include "What The Moon Saw", "Heaven Tonight (starring John Waters and Guy Pearce). "Hunting" (starring American star John Savage), "Beyond My Reach", and "Flynn" (starring Guy Pearce, Claudia Karvan, and Steven Berkoff). These films and others were sold to Miramax, Paramount, American Broadcasting Corporation, Disney, Warners, Skouras, J & M Entertainment, Village Roadshow, Hoyts and screened all over the world. In 1989 Howson was awarded the Producer of the Year Award by Film Victoria, and since then has received several Hall of

Fame Awards and Lifetime Achievement Awards by various international film festivals. As a result of this acclaim Howson lived and worked in Hollywood for nine years. Over the past decade he has turned his attention to the theatre and directed the Australia premiere of Caryl Churchill's play "A Number" to great critical and commercial success. Due to its success it was revived 12 months later for a return season. He has written the Rhonda Burchmore hit one-womn show "Cry Me A River - The World of Julie London), as well as ghost writing Ms. Burchmore's best-selling autobiography, "Legs 11." Recently he has written and directed two sell-out seasons of the hit show "Genesis To Broadway." His latest award winning feature film "Remembering Nigel" stars Martin Landau, Sally Kirkland, Steven Berkoff, Tyler Hilton, Thea Gill, Mark Rydell, Eric Burdon, Michael J. Pollard, Alex Scott, John Savage, P.F. Sloan and many other international names. His musical based on the life of Bobby Darin, "Dream Lover" has its world premiere in Sydney, Australia, September 2016.

facebook.com/frank.howson
frankhowson.com
frankhowsonblog.wordpress.com

Photo & Illustration Credits

17 - pic by VANESSA ALLAN
19 - pic by VANESSA ALLAN
31 - pic by BARRY ROBINSON
37 - pic by OLIVER HOWSON
47 - pic by FRANK HOWSON
55 - pic by RAIJA REISSENBERGER
59 - pic by BARRY ROBINSON
73 - pic by FRANK HOWSON
79 - pic by FRANK HOWSON
85 - painting by PATTI REES
91 - pic by VANESSA ALLAN
97 - sketch by FRANK HOWSON
101 - pic by FRANK HOWSON
105 - pic by BARRY ROBINSON
111 - pic by RAIJA REISENBERGER
121 - sketch by FRANK HOWSON
127 - pic by JOANNE FRANCIS
135 - pic by MICHAEL TOWNE
145 - pic by FRANK HOWSON
151 - pic by VANESSA ALLAN
155 - pic by VANESA ALLAN
161 - pic by FRANK HOWSON
165 - pic by FRANK HOWSON
173 - pic by LUNA PARK PRODUCTIONS
175 - pic by FRANK HOWSON
178 - pic by FRANK HOWSON
181 - sketch by FRANK HOWSON
184 - sketch by FRANK HOWSON
187 - pic by FRANK HOWSON
192 - pic by VANESSA ALLAN
196 - sketch by FRANK HOWSON
199 - pic by MILES BENNETT
203 - pic by PEARL HOWSON

206 - pic by CHRISTINE WALTERS
210 - pic by PEARL HOWSON
213 - pic by FRANK HOWSON
216 - pic by FRANK HOWSON
219 - pic by FRANK HOWSON
226 - sketch by FRAN HOWSON
229 - pic by MICHAEL TOWNE
230 - sketch by FRANK HOWSON
234 - pic by FRANK HOWSON
239 - pic by OLIVER HOWSON
245 - sketch by FRANK HOWSON
250 - sketch by FRANK HOWSON
257 - sketch by FRANK HOWSON
259 - sketch by FRAN HOWSON
265 - sketch by FRANK HOWSON
271 - pic by PEARL HOWSON
274 - sketch by FRANK HOWSON
284 - pic by FRANK HOWSON
286 - pic by J. MARSHALL CRAIG
289 - pic by HENRY HOWSON
293 - sketch by FRANK HOWSON
294 - sketch by FRANK HOWSON
298 - pic by FRANK HOWSON
307 - pic by MILES BENNETT
311 - pic by FRANK HOWSON
313 - pic by VANESSA ALLAN
317 - sketch by FRANK HOWSON
319 - pic by PEARL HOWSON

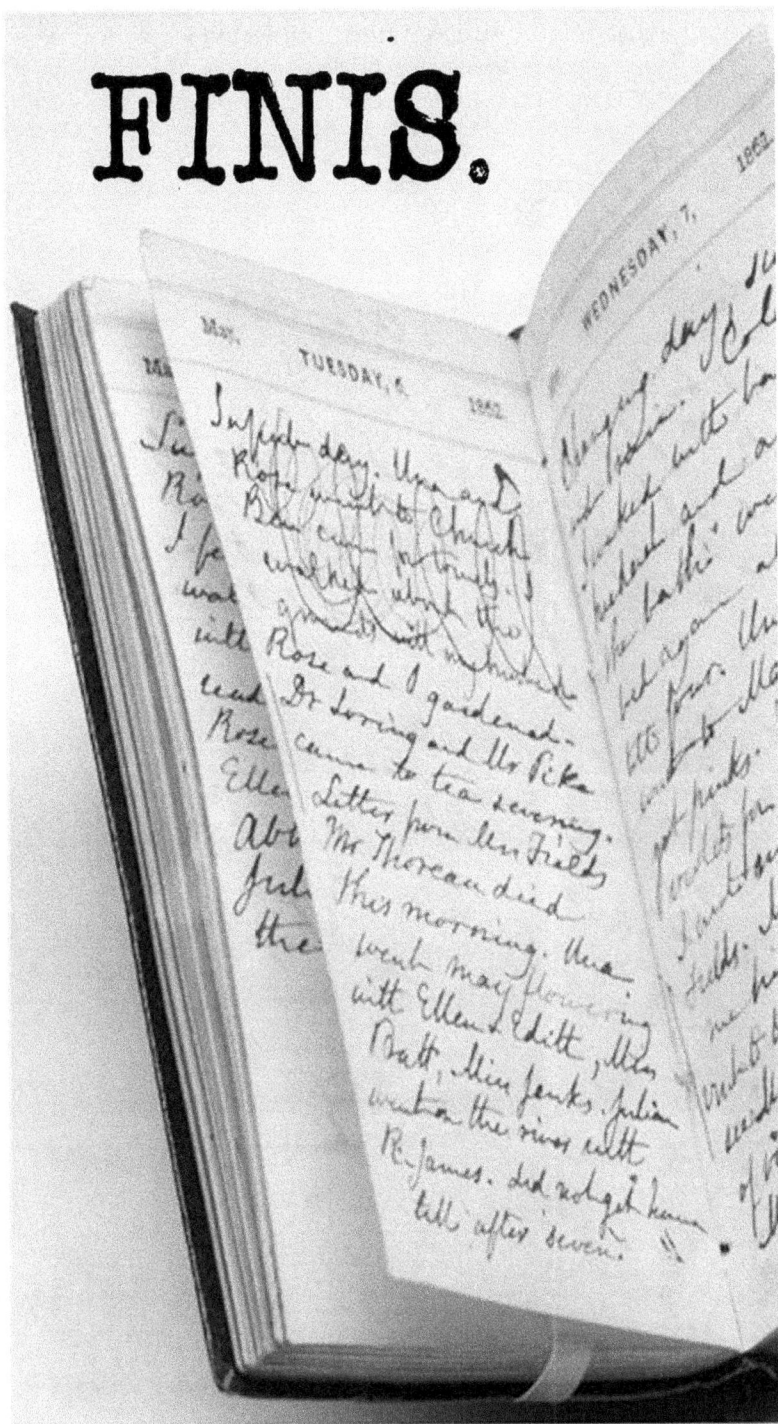

Also from Quill & Quire Publishers

www.quillandquirepublishers.com

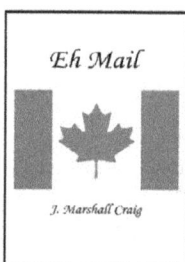

The Long Way Home

www.ingramcontent.com/pod-product-compliance
Lightning Source LLC
Chambersburg PA
CBHW060001100426
42740CB00010B/1365